Ron Sardanopoli

Leap of Trust

Leap of Trust

....

An inspirational true story about an inner-city youths' plight of perseverance during a disruptive decade of social poverty, burning buildings, homelessness, street gangs, and crime.

Ron Sardanopoli

Ron Sardanopoli

ISBN 9781688418554

For my wife Linda who has blessed me with 48 wonderful years of marriage filled with love and affection. We are blessed with a son and a daughter Renaldo and Danielle, five grandchildren, Valentino, Leonardo, Madison, Lucas, and Mia. Linda supported me during my 36 years of military service as a military wife, and supported me to work after hours to help an inner-city youth find a better path in life.

Table of Contents

Leap of Trust

Preface

During the entire decade of the 1970's the Southern borough of the Bronx in New York City was turned into a decayed community. There were burning apartment buildings, vacant abandoned buildings, jobless tenants that were unable to pay their rent. This led to a higher homeless rate because of many of those that once had housing and could not pay rent became homeless. When the apartment buildings in the South Bronx became filled with homeless tenants that could no longer pay their rent, and eviction notices were not affective to evict them, the wealthy building owners became desperate. Landlords and their torch men put together a murderous wave of arson where landlords profited by collecting insurance money to make up for their loss of tenant rental income. There were no codes in place where city or state were able to stop this fire epidemic. This ruthless wave to deal with the tenants ran rampant. By the mid 1970's many believed 40 percent of the South Bronx apartment buildings were burned to the ground. It was a sight comparable to bombed-out towns and cities during World War II battle sites. The South Bronx was

in a physical and economic turmoil. While this decade reached economic recession, these meticulous looks of destruction were signs of economic depression conditions, and eventually turned the South Bronx into a crime invested area. State and Government turned their backs to this for a long while, Washington wanted New York City and New York State to fix it self. New York City was entering a state of bankruptcy, and had no funds to offer. Politics added more sludge to the possibilities of fixing the problem. Cultural street gangs started popping up to rule their own turf, eventually the streets of the South Bronx crime rates multiplied. Street gangs' main source of income was drug dealing, robberies of small convenience stores, purse snatching, and car stripping, to name a few. This led to hundreds of thousands of middle-class people that lived in the Bronx to flee and move to suburban neighborhoods away from the Bronx. The South Bronx quickly changed from a multi-cultural area into an area where the majority were African Americans and Puerto Ricans. The German, Irish, and Italian families headed to the suburban neighborhoods that fostered more safe communities. Many youths were forced to make a decision on how to survive the streets of the South Bronx. There were not many positive paths remaining for a youth that lived in a poverty-stricken South Bronx. This book is about one of those youths that was raised and stayed in this arson epidemic, caused by a total economic collapse. He was unable to make the move for a better lifestyle, or maybe he just didn't know how?

From 1970 to 1978 I traveled through the streets of the South Bronx just about every day to my workplace when I was employed with the New York Army National Guard. I could not fathom being a youth growing up in these living conditions. I was always mesmerized when I viewed the torn down South Bronx while traveling through the streets. My sincere compassion for the underprivileged human beings has always been my daunting and most difficult unsettling subject matter to deal with. It makes me wonder, if I can just make a difference by guiding a youth away from this poverty-stricken lifestyle. If there was a way, I could help a youth make a better life for himself, I would do it. But how would I know? Where is this youth? How can I add more free time away from my career and my family to help someone? Can I get a signal or a sign that could lead me to a situation where I could help?

One afternoon around early November 1976 while I was at my workplace in the South Bronx district of New York City, my desk phone rang. A New York City Police Officer was on the other end. He wanted to know if I was Warrant Officer Ron Sardanopoli. I said, "yes I am," He said, "my name is Police Officer Smith from the 41st Precinct." He went on and said, "a youth is with me now and claims to know you. He claims to be in the same military organization as yours. I'm getting ready to make multiple arrests for a street gang robbery. One youth, by the name of Jimmy Gomez has a different alibi than the rest and he specifically only trusted you to verify his background information." After my conversation with Smith, I said to myself, "Is this my calling? Am I being summonsed to be that good Samaritan to help a street youth?" It was this phone call that began this journey, an incredible inspirational true story about a youth with insurmountable courage and perseverance, that was born and raised in the streets of the South Bronx. You will learn more about him and the avenue he chooses in his search for a path to distance

himself from the hood, and find a future that could lead him to economic success and to be a conscientious citizen.

CHAPTER 1

South Bronx

A street kid that surrounds himself with his social demons is searching for an escape that will release him from his fears, anger and stress that is bottled up inside him. His fear of poverty, burning tenement buildings, crime, street gangs, homeless and the police, are real life concerns for youths living in the South Bronx during the 1970's. This horrific decade left him no choice but to battle his inner emotions, and the unavoidable violence that illuminates the surroundings of his everyday life. This street youth is special, because he already understands that life has more to offer than the one, he is being dealt. He also has an incredible ability to bob and weave many dangerous situations that his life in the streets throw at him. But how long can he avoid the dangers that lurks before him

day in and day out? What chances does a South Bronx youth have to escape this poverty-stricken lifestyle and reach any kind of economic success?

This tale took place during a small window of time, in the South Bronx during the horrific decade of the 1970's. These living conditions are not supposed to happen to any of our American citizens, but it did. It happened to the people living in the South Bronx during this decade. it literally spread like "wild fire." From the early 1970's to the end of 1979 thousands of apartment buildings and houses were lost to arson, crime soared. By the mid-1970s, the Bronx, New York murder rate had nearly tripled in just five years, with more total murders than the entire city of New York sees today. Children were mugged in the street. Hundreds of thousands of middle-class residents fled to the suburbs to escape this decaying South Bronx. The people who stayed behind disproportionately depended on welfare and public housing to survive. This street kid was one of the thousands of youths left behind to survive the hood. He stood behind and it was no choice of his own, he had to ride out this poverty-stricken area holding his head high as best he can. Many of the left behind youths who were born and raised in this crime infested area of the South Bronx community had to choose a path to survive. Some were successful, but many were not, especially those who fell because of the demons that poverty areas create for them.

During this time period the South Bronx was avoided at all costs. It became one of the poorest districts of New York City, and possibly the entire country. The area became an arson epidemic caused by the total economic collapse. It was a time when landlords and their torch men put together a murderous wave of arson, where landlords profited. It was a time when policies or building codes that existed by the state did not stop landlords to continue to profit from burning down their buildings. This area where most of this very real story takes place is located in the heart of the Morrisania community in the South Bronx. During the 1970's this area was a symbol of urban decay. More concerning is it took an entire decade for our State and Government leaders to create a chance for those left behind. After living ten years of oppression, poverty, homeless, and shame, how can the citizens make up this lost time in their life's? The kids raised in these streets during this decade had a major disadvantage in living their life compared to the many financial stable communities in New York City, and the USA. Their immediate surroundings find ways to derail their day to day life. Many of the kids in these neighborhoods have fallen by taking part in gang violence, stealing, drug dealing, drug use, and eventually jail time or even death due to crime or drugs.

New York City was thought of at this time as a glamorous updated clean metropolitan tourist attraction at a national level in the 1970's. But the truth is the South Bronx section of New York City during this time was a social disaster. The population that lived in the South Bronx district during this time was predominantly African American, and Hispanic. Those that lived in this area during this timeframe will all tell you that the conditions were not so glamorous, conditions were more horrific, is the best description. Starting from the early 1970's, Government, States, were hoping that the Mayor of New York City can hopefully fix itself. But when poverty began spreading to the North Bronx, more middleclass citizens began fleeing to the suburbs to escape the Bronx by the hundreds of thousands.

On October 16, 1975, New York City was deep in crisis. At 4 P.M. the next day, four hundred and fifty-three million dollars of the city's debts would come due, but there were only thirty-four million dollars on hand. If New York couldn't pay those debts, the city would officially be bankrupt. The largest city in the United States was heading for bankruptcy. That was when the Government began paying attention. The immediate crisis averted; New York's politicians and leaders continued to petition for federal help. Twelve days later, President Ford stepped to the podium at the National Press Club and delivered a stinging rebuke. "What I cannot understand—and what nobody should condone—is the blatant attempt in some quarters to frighten the American people and their representatives in Congress into panicky support of patently bad policy. The people of this country will not be stampeded; they will not panic when a few desperate New York City officials and bankers try to scare New York's mortgage payments out of them." Later in the speech, he added, "I can tell you, and tell you now, that I am prepared to veto any bill that has as its purpose a federal bailout of New York City to prevent a default."'

Ironically, Ford's tough words, and the even tougher headline they engendered, may have served to save New York and sink Ford. For New York, Ford's statement convinced the key players that no federal help would be forthcoming. It galvanized the city to make tough choices and significant changes. Rubenstein, Koch, and others would later say that by refusing to save the city, Ford did the city a service. (For better or worse, it may also have enshrined brinkmanship as a bankruptcy negotiating tactic.) which is the practice of trying to achieve an advantageous outcome by pushing dangerous events to the brink of active conflict.

And although Ford would later approve federal support for New York, New Yorkers remembered the headline, that Ford denied to help New York City. The following year, Jimmy Carter received the third-highest vote share a Democratic presidential candidate ever received in New York City, narrowly won New York State, and with it, the forty-one electoral votes that give him the Presidency—revealing the impact from one speech that wasn't given, and one that was.

President Carter with his staff visiting South Bronx, New York 1977, to eye witness the total devastation of burned down buildings.

This photo above with our President at the time and his staff to include its back drop of devastation became a historical photo that helped convince Washington and the rest of our nation, that the South Bronx is burning, and needs help. Take a look at the background landscape; this was only a small sample of how bad the conditions were in the South Bronx. I remember when President Carter visited the South Bronx. I watched this on television news. Our President got his show and tell tour of the South Bronx, by New York's senior political leaders. At the time the President was briefed that these conditions that he is viewing around him exists in 40% of the buildings of the South Bronx. Think about 40 percent of the buildings in the borough of the largest city in the United States burned down to the ground. An eerie thought to say the least. The President could not believe the devastation and how it existed for so long. In today's time, when any major destruction caused by tornados, and hurricanes, and fires happened to any of our City or States, the President quickly announces a National Disaster. Immediate federal funds become available from Federal Emergency Management Agency – FEMA for relief to our citizens. Other states send volunteer firemen, carpenters, etc. on a humanitarian mission to help. This destruction did not get this kind of urgency, the South Bronx needed immediate attention. President Regan followed up on President Carters plan to rebuild the South Bronx. Positive signs of economic recovery had not affected the citizens of the South Bronx until the early 1980's. By this time, it was estimated that 90% of the buildings were burned down to the ground. With the building of new single-family homes, town houses and condo's the housing in the South Bronx began to build back their population, and with the tougher crack-down on crime coupled with more public housing units and suburban type homes being built, giving the South Bronx a face lift, and economic boost. The South Bronx began experiencing a social come back.

People that survived this decade were hurt, both physically and mentally. For the American citizens that had to live in the South Bronx during this horrific decade, it was too late for them to recuperate their losses. This left the citizens of South Bronx to live an entire decade of economic carnage. Homeless shelters were created all around New York City. The New York City armories became converted to homeless shelters. The rebuild plan did not help the population of the South Bronx until many years after President Carter visited the South Bronx. This left behind a massive population of American citizens that were tarnished by being raised in this decade of distorted devastating. In many cases, it was too late for the youths that grew up in this era of the South Bronx to redevelop proper cognitive skills to compete. Their confidence to compete against the privileged youth that did not experience this distorted lifestyle, was unconscionable. The youths in the South Bronx were negatively affected by the devastation at many levels with housing, healthcare, jobless rates, and their education. The high school dropout rate soared during the 1970's. Many students that attended public schools in the South Bronx were homeless, after school they went home to shelters. Many had to drop out of high school because of their living conditions. There were insurmountable numbers of young adults who did not complete their high school education. Their living conditions were demoralizing and this weak economy contributed to jobless tenants, burned down buildings, proliferation of gang violence and drugs. Unfair distribution of education funds was noticeable by the conditions of the public-school system located in these decayed communities. The South Bronx public schools and their students were being left behind by this dropping economic tail spin. Those who survived living these conditions found a positive path for their family and themselves, deserve credit beyond recognition. Will the demons of this young man's

community during this decade win the battle to derail his path to be economically successful? Will he take a chance to lift himself above his plight for a more positive future?

Chapter 2

Economic Recession

My alarm clock goes off at 5:30am as it does every morning, all showered and ready to go to work. My home is located in a town called Stormville. Stormville is located outside New York City in Dutchess County. Its outdoor surroundings are filled with tranquil mountains and trees filled with the fresh mountain air, breezes that provide the aroma of wild pine trees, and cut grass. The early morning sounds of beautiful variations of birds chirping and squirrels scampering through the dead leaves. The occasional wild turkey sightings, and deer's trotting through the trails that are created by themselves through their life cycle. Our new living digs was such a wonderful relaxing, and safe change from living in the Bronx, New

York. It's a place for my family to grow together, and our new place that we called home.

I embraced this change, and our new living experience mainly because the economic recession of this decade began deteriorating our neighborhoods in the Bronx. I was born and raised in the tough streets of the North Bronx, in New York City, at the time it was predominantly an Italian cultured neighborhood (nick named: Little Italy), 187th Street was the main street that ran the center of the length of our neighborhood. During the years that my siblings and I was raised in the Bronx, the economics was at a healthy state. During the 1950's the economy experienced a shift that created more income for more Americans than ever before. During the 1960's the United States experienced its longest uninterrupted period of economic expansion in history. In the 1960's housing and the computer industry overpowered the industry. The education system was firing on all pistons, there was enough teachers employed to handle the volumes of students that lived in the local communities. It was safe to walk the streets of our neighborhoods. Families stayed out on the stoops of their buildings, fire escapes, and roof tops of our buildings. These outdoor locations were a way to gather and bond with neighbors. Our healthy economy during the 1950's and 1960's allowed families throughout America a chance to attain economic success.

I was raised by my immigrant parents who were born and raised in Rionero, Italy, a small town outside the city of Potenza, Italy. Mom and Dad were employed and all of my siblings were employed during their decades of growth. All of my siblings including myself were born in America, we became the first generation of Americans. My four brothers, from oldest to youngest, Mauro (recently deceased) a major loss to our family, and to our society. He was a United States Army Chief Warrant Officer retired, and a forty-year Army veteran. The next is Anthony who was a successful Wall Street Coffee and Cocoa trader, also an Army Veteran who served a two-year tour for the United States Army, stationed in Germany during the Vietnam War era. The next is Robert a retired bank manager. He completed six-year service with the Army National Guard with an honorable discharge. Armando, our family retired chemical engineer, hired by a blue-chip company BASF, and tasked to a two-year overseas tour as a team leader in Holland, he learned the German language to brief his senior officials. Today Armando is passing on his engineering technical knowledge, as he is teaching plastics technology at the Schoolcraft College in Livonia, Michigan. I'm revealing my family history during this time because this was a time when economics was healthy and jobs were more available. A time when families grew together and developed strong family bonds, compared to the 1970's. This was a time when a family can put together a plan to stay above the poverty level. It was our economic conditions combined with secure housing and a strong family bond that helped us reach economic success. Our richness that we received from our family plan were gifts of faith, love, hope, and family.

During the 1970's the stock market was a mess, economic growth was weak resulting in rising unemployment that eventually reached double digits. The economic recession during the decade of the 1970's could not give the people living in the South Bronx the same opportunities as those that lived there during the 1950's and 60's. The phrase "The Bronx is burning" attributed to a very popular sports announcer by the name of Howard Cosell during Game 2 of the 1977 World Series featuring the New York Yankees and Los Angeles Dodgers. Howard Cosell was referring to a helicopter aerial view of buildings burning around Yankee Stadium in the South Bronx. The aerial view showed the arson epidemic caused by the total economic collapse of the South Bronx during the 1970's. Everyday buildings were on fire, people died, the families with their children were moving from place to place, disrupting their day to day activities of employment, education, etc., a total loss of family stability. Community infrastructure was affected, hospitals, social services, and schools became weakened.

Eventually I became a statistic and fled the Bronx, headed north in New York to suburbia to start our family. The only drawback to this move was that I had to travel a long distance to my workplace in the South Bronx. During my commute from home to work, the transition from the country views, the quality of air and sounds of our home, compared to the South Bronx's was like leaving paradise and entering a World War II bombed out war zone. The South Bronx became a deteriorating poverty-stricken area. When I traveled to my workplace every day, the streets landscape looked horrific. I would slow my car down to view the devastation of the landscape. The buildings and infrastructure that were standing were decaying, and the buildings became deteriorated. At this time, it was reported by the media, forty percent of the buildings in the South Bronx were burned to the ground. Reports indicate buildings were burned down using gasoline. Many finishers became extremely rich by buying properties from struggling landlords, this artificially drove up the value, insuring them and then burning them. The properties were still occupied by subsidized tenants or squatters at the time, who were given short or no warning before the building was burnt down. They were forced to move to another slum building where the

process would usually repeat itself. The rate of unsolved fatalities due to fire multiplied sevenfold in the South Bronx, with many residents reporting being burnt out of numerous apartment blocks one after the other. Driving hundreds of thousands of people from their homes and injuring and killing thousands more.

Youths watching firemen battle a blaze of a burning building in the South Bronx during the 1970's.

Some believe that local South Bronx residents themselves also burned down vacant properties in their own neighborhoods. Much of this was reportedly done by those who had already worked stripping and burning

buildings for pay. The ashes of burned down properties could be sifted for salable scrap metal. Other fires were caused by unsafe electrical wiring, fires set indoors for heating, and random vandalism associated with the general crime situation. I remember watching small groups of homeless men and woman finding ways to keep warm, or searching in garbage pails for their next meal. Using shopping carts to transport their clothes, or stuff that was valuable to them to survive on the streets. The homeless were taking a chance to use the vacant buildings that were getting ready to be demolished. These vacant buildings became their shelter. The large number of vacant buildings attracted squatters, drug dealers and addicts.

Eventually they were burned down, the bricks and all its remaining constructions items, remained there and it almost seemed forever. The entire landscape appearance in the South Bronx looked like something out of a bombed-out city of a World War II movie. It seemed forever that the debris from these torn down buildings got cleaned up. It was an epic view; I felt at times the views were larger than life. To witness so much devastation, I felt saddened and angry for the citizens of the South Bronx, their human lives were trapped to live this lifestyle. While traveling and stopping at a traffic light, homeless men/boys of all ages, without asking permission, stationed themselves by a traffic light and once the traffic light turned red, they would run up to the vehicle's windshield with a bucket of dirty over used water. Using a hand held sponge/squidgy to soak the car windows quickly in an effort to clean the car windshield before the light turns green. They had to time it to finish before the light turned green, and hopefully the driver of the vehicle would appreciate their work, or just for a way to help the homeless and give them a monetary tip. Some of the people that had to survive this decade in the South Bronx during these desperate times used these kinds of desperate measures for a way of income. This was one of the ways where the homeless people could make money. The New York City Police seemed to allow this, if they became a nuisance the police would just have them removed, where they continue their work on another street corner with a stop sign or a traffic light. The South Bronx is located in the richest city in the world, and part of the richest countries in the world. Why is this happening? Who is to blame? Where are our city and state politicians and leaders when you need them?

Ghost town streets and neighborhoods, it was extremely dangerous, mysterious, and exciting at the same time. I became a rubber necker, I couldn't help thinking that we live in a nation that has the technology and finance to send people to the moon, and yet they allow our own citizens in this rich country to live this way. The vibrant street life, the rebellious spirit, the scenes of destruction all around, and the constant fear of being mugged made my daily visits to the South Bronx unpredictable and memorable at the same time. Whenever I drove or walked the streets of the South Bronx, I encountered many levels of suspicion, anger and confusion. People who lived in the South Bronx didn't know where the next blow was coming from. I always wondered how difficult it must be for hard working; stand up citizens to raise a family in such a horrible environment, with terrible social conditions. A place where many youths can get caught up by making bad decisions. What chances do they have to grow into healthy, successful, educated men or women? If there was just some way or somehow that I could play a role into helping someone lift their spirits and provide support and guidance to get them to a positive path.

During this decade the South Bronx property values continued to plummet to record lows. A vicious cycle began to where large number of tenements and multi-story, multifamily apartment buildings (left vacant by white flight). These structures stood vacant and unsalable, an existence of a stagnant economy and an extremely high unemployment rate. This was the perfect cocktail for street gangs, and drug dealers.

The neighborhoods of the entire south Bronx during the 1970's harvested some of the toughest neighborhood street gangs. The names of these gangs were mentioned on the local news for crime activity. Drug dealers ran rapport in the South Bronx. Drive-bys were just beginning to become a popular gang activity. Some of the names of the gangs from the South Bronx at the time were the Black Spades, Savage Skulls, Savage Nomads, Screaming Phantoms. There were many other organized smaller gangs with less manpower, but the ones mentioned had

numbers reaching the hundreds in manpower. The larger gangs were more popular and seemed to rule most of the territories in the South Bronx. These neighborhoods that harvested these street gangs were policed by New York's finest. The area had five police stations to provide security to the pedestrians of the South Bronx. Those precincts are 40th, 41st, 42nd, 44th, and the 48th. The South Bronx is New York 's 15th Congressional District for the United States House of Representatives. One of the most popular precincts with the highest crime rate arrests was the 41st, nicknamed "Fort Apache." Those who worked in the Fort Apache district had to endure the fear and corruption of their surroundings. For these police officers, it felt like working in an army outpost in foreign territory. The streets were filled with some of the worst and dangerous gangs, criminals, and drug dealers. After the Germans, Irish, Jewish and Italians moved out to join the flight, Hispanics made up a majority of this area's population followed by African Americans.

I often thought about, what chances a teenage boy has being raised in these neighborhoods of the South Bronx. Their lifestyle class reaching poverty levels; unemployment is at its all-time high. Their education level and the level of children being educated in these poverty-stricken neighborhoods were below standard for some compared to rest of the state's education level. The South Bronx property values continued to plummet; deteriorated buildings were demolished. The South Bronx reached economic stagnation, poverty, and urban decay. The entire New York City began feeling the deep tail spin provoked by the flight of the middle class to the suburbs.

In the South Bronx, the nationwide economic recession hit New York's industrial sector especially hard. The streets were dirty, with beer cans, and liquor bottles, scattered with household garbage. The schools looked deteriorated, broken windows by youths throwing objects to destroy property. Abandoned buildings were decayed the homeless would take over these empty buildings. Places to sell drugs, and gangs would battle for their territories to own territories day in and day out. Young people were involved in making wrong choices because of their environment. A culture erupted in the South Bronx that was separate from mainstream America, hidden from government to protect American values. Men gambling throwing dice, most street signs were torn and lots of faded advertisements. Cars stripped to its frame, sitting up on cement blocks to steal the tires and parts. Homeless men and women, trying to keep warm by hovering around a fire built in the steel garbage pails that were stationed in front of these destroyed buildings for

their tenants that once lived there. To keep the fire roaring they used building material from the empty tenement buildings. A horrific culture has erupted.

Chapter 3

Trouble Follows

When I traveled the streets of the South Bronx in my vehicle, and I came to a stop sign or a traffic light where at times, I had to stop my vehicle near youths getting loud, drinking alcohol, I always did a 360-visual safety check. I placed my safety first when traveling through the ghost town streets of these neighborhoods. Hearing and reading about a street thug trying to gain access to vehicles, car jack or just a hold up. Yes, I had respect for these neighborhoods. Walking alone in neighborhoods controlled by street gangs wearing my civilian attire during the evening hours was something that I tried to avoid. But when I did wind up in those situations and I ran into groups of teenagers, I experienced shouting out of various negative comments directed at me. I was an

unknown person walking their turf. I was once told by chattering youths, “We know you’re an undercover NYPD” I thought that was interesting observation by them, but I would continue to walk briskly past the heckling crowd. Sometimes the actual words they used were more volatile. All their comments made me feel that I was not wanted in their neighborhoods. Very rarely did I see police officers patrolling these torn down side streets. Growing up in the Bronx, I totally understood boundaries, especially when it came to different cultural neighborhoods during the evening hours. All neighborhoods were extremely protective of their territory. It was the way of life in the streets of the Bronx.

One early afternoon while at work, I decided to take my vehicle to pick up lunch for myself and some coworkers. At the end of my drive back to the armory I had an everlasting life experience. As I pulled up to the only guarded entrance by two state employees who work for

the state as building maintenance and unarmed security men. I drove my car to a driveway that leads to a secured steel rollup door. In order to gain access to drive my vehicle into the secured armory, the protocol is to get out of my car, ring a bell to alert the maintenance men that a vehicle is requesting to gain access into the armory. This location of 168th Street and Franklin Avenue at the time had a torn down building across the street from the steel door, and the remaining buildings standing were beginning to show signs of tenants leaving and buildings being vacated. This street becomes a ghost town street in the evening, and not many people tend to walk through this street. After ringing the bell, a maintenance/security man has to walk about thirty yards from his observation room to the inside section of the steel roll up door. He first looks through a peep hole to recognize the person requesting access into the armory before he allows them

access. After I step out of my vehicle to ring the bell, I secured myself back into my vehicle. I waited for the security state employee to walk to the door and peak out to notice that I was the one who rang the bell. While in my car waiting for the steel door to open, I usually keep my eyes focused on the peep hole waiting for a security person to let me in. I notice the maintenance/security employee looking through the peep hole to see if it was safe for him to open the door. What was strange, the maintenance man kept on looking but never opened the door? He must see something that concerns him. Thinking to myself, "he knows me, he knows my car, and he knew I left the armory to pick up lunch. So why is he not opening the steel door to let me in?" While waiting in my car, staring directly at the peep hole with the eyeball moving around, I began doing my 360-degree safety scan around my car with my windows rolled up and doors locked, I noticed a very tall man with a leather type gang vest in

the rear of my driver's side. When he noticed that I noticed him, he approached the driver's side of my window coming from the rear of my car, his hands were folded in front of him looking like an innocent bystander, he asked me, "can I ask you a question?" Being so close to the armory at the time, I didn't feel this person was a threat. I wasn't going to make him feel that he is a threat especially because it's the middle of the day. So, I rolled down the window about half way and asked him, "What can I do for you?" and faster than you can imagine, this guy pulled back his black leather vest and placed his right hand on the handgrip of his gun, that was tucked in his right side of his pants with the barrel facing down. I freaked out, now looking straight ahead, taking short breaths, hoping the steel door would open, wondering why the steel door has not opened, I noticed in a brief look that the eyeball of the guard was still visible, and that is why he is not opening the door. I was frightened that my life was going to end. This perpetrator did not say one word. Maybe he was waiting for the guard to open the steel rollup door to gain illegal access. So, I yelled, "What do you want?" My heart was beating a mile a minute and there was no response from the gunman. At the time, I was driving my personal Chevrolet Camaro, a sports vehicle. Because of the design of my car, my bucket seat was low to the ground with the hardtop separating my view to the man's face, but the weapon tucked in his trouser was very visible, with his right hand and the handle. I didn't want to make any sudden moves or head movement to make him think I was going to retaliate. I wasn't sure now if he just wanted to shoot me, or did he want to gain access into the armory where we store weapons and ammunition.

I began gaining my senses back from this sudden frightening event. My military basic training kicked in and

remembered the Code of the U.S. Fighting Force. What to do in this situation when the enemy is trying to capture you. For those that had no military training, the code of conduct is an ethics guide and a United States Department of Defense directive consisting of six articles to members of the United States Armed Forces. Article III states, "If I am captured, I will continue to resist by all means available. I will make all efforts to escape and aid others to escape. I will accept neither parole nor special favors from the enemy." The basic meaning of this code is, the longer one takes to make the move to escape, the more confidence the enemy gains to be able to contain his hostage. In my case once that steel door opens, the gunman gains access into the armory. I don't know if he had others with him in a close by proximity to drive their getaway car into the armory behind me. My heart is palpitating a mile a minute, sweat was beading down my

forehead, my left hand is gripped tightly on the steering wheel and my right hand was resting on my automatic shifter located in the middle of the console.

Before I go on to tell you the outcome of this frightening event, let me share another event that started pretty much the same way, and its outcome. With all the street gangs, crimes, organized crimes that became a way of life in the urban areas of the Bronx, and crime began spreading outside these neighborhoods, there was a successful attempt during this decade to rob weapons and ammunition at a State Armory prior to this. It took place on November 29, 1971 around 3PM according to the police. Four men dressed in military clothing one of them wearing a Navy pea coat were armed with pistols and rifles invaded the New York State Armory on North Broadway in Yonkers, New York. These four men escaped with eight M-16 semi-automatic rifles, and 3,000 rounds of M16A1 ammunition. These gun men fired no shots but locked eight Army National Guard troops and two armory maintenance/security men in a room after striking one of the maintenance/security men in the head with the butt of a rifle. The victim maintenance/security man said, "the perpetrator struck me because I was not moving fast enough before he struck him in the head with the butt of the rifle." The guardsmen and the two maintenance men on duty at the time were forced at gunpoint into a basement weapons room. That is the location where the M-16 rifles and ammunition were collected and the 10 men were left inside.

I thought at this time, he was doing it to gain access into the armory, and eventually to steal the weapons and ammunition. My car had a box frame shifter; all I had to do is squeeze the shifter with my right-hand finger tips to unlock the shifter, and move the shifter to reverse and give it gas. The gear shifter was hidden from the perpetrator and reverse was my only option, moving my shifter to the drive position would make me crash into the steel door. My heart was beating faster and faster. It felt like my head was going to explode. I never was up against this kind of life death situation. I said to myself, it's now or never, in one motion, I press my shifter to release it from the park position, and pushed the shifter back to reverse while at the same time slamming my right foot to the gas pedal all the way down to the floor.

My rear wheels were screaming, and peeling rubber that created black smoke and loud screeching sounds. My car rear wheels immediately jumped the curb across the street from the armory side, and I suddenly hit the brakes. I saw quickly that the perpetrator looked at my direction after my rear tire's car jumped the curb. A woman screaming at me because, I frighten her as she was walking the sidewalk across the street where my car jumped the curb. The perpetrator ran about ten steps and turned right at the corner to run down an adjacent avenue. I lost visual sight of him. I put my breaks on in time to avoid a woman and her baby in a carriage that were untouched. There was a corner building, still erected, not demolished by fire located directly across the street from the State Armory access steel door. I was extremely apologetic to this unharmed mom. I asked her if she was ok. She said, yes, I'm ok, and also at the same time just furious because of the entire event that upset her. I continue to make sure she was ok, after she calmed down, I asked her if she witness a man that just ran around the corner? She didn't want any part of being a witness, and quickly walked away from it all. Being a witness to a potential street crime is a big no-no to the citizens of their communities. I suspect the perpetrator ran, because that woman was an eye witness to a possible crime. Realizing now why the gun man ran and the maintenance/security man didn't open the door for me. The maintenance man that looked through the peep hole on the door told me he saw a stranger standing by my door, he didn't recognize him so he didn't open the door. He said, "I didn't want to open this rollup door in case that person wanted to gain illegal access to the armory. He also said, "I will call the police to file a report." I told him, "the streets of the South Bronx are dangerous anytime of the day, it's just crazy out here." More importantly the security protocol to gain access into the armory was successful, and the maintenance/security guards did their job and prevented a possible unauthorized access to a gunman.

Chapter 4

A Citizen Soldier

The New York Army National is comprised of dedicated citizen soldiers. These soldiers are everyday people, some live in the local community and some lived outside the community. These soldiers belong to a military organization located in an armory, each armory shelters an Army military organization, sometimes more than one organization. The organization that was sheltered at the time in this specific South Bronx Armory had an Army designation of, 1st Battalion 105th Field Artillery. This armory is located on 168th street, and Franklin Ave, Bronx, New York, directly in the heart of the South Bronx, Morrisania section. This was where I was employed, and is where Jimmy Gomez reported for duty as a citizen soldier.

This armory was constructed back in the early 1900's to look like an accent castle. Today New York City now uses this armory as a homeless shelter. I was always attracted to the gothic appearance of the outside and the inside structure. This was the first permanent armory located in The Bronx. It was built in three years from 1908 to 1911, and was designed by a man called Charles C Haight. Mr. Haight who was a former member of the New York State militia and a prominent architect known for his institutional buildings. This armory was situated on a sloping site. Its structure has bold brick forms, picturesque, yet it pronounces a very powerful force design, in the same time always retaining references to the tradition of medieval times. Compared to all of the building designs in the New York City area, this armory stands alone a design that attracts so much flare, and interest from people that have interests in the Gothics architecture, and history. The armory has a large drill shed and an administrative building to the side, anchored by a corner tower; the armory was critically praised for its rational structural expression. The medieval appearance helped to signify the armory as a distinct building type, connoted its military function, as well as the concepts of power and control. The armory's structure highlights its look of power and control with its detail appearance. For example, it features turrets, towers, battlements, slit windows, impenetrable doors, and window grilles. All of which could be used by troops with guns or to thwart uninvited enemy. The local and distant community soldiers that were stationed to this armory were mostly the very soldiers you hear about on the news or read about who put their lives on hold from their civilian lives to defend aid and protect our state and great nation. They have developed through the years and sometimes labeled as part time soldiers or weekend warrior during peace time. These labels have to do with the scheduling of soldier training. Army National Guard soldiers trained one weekend a month, and two weeks during the summer months. There is a skeleton fulltime staff that keeps the armories up to date for administrative, logistics, training, and maintenance purposes. Armories also had state employees that provided maintenance and security to

The South Bronx, New York State Armory used as a home station to conduct Army National Guard Administrative, Training and Logistics readiness missions.

the facility. The federal soldiers/employees are hired to be available 24/7 in case the Army National Guard is called out on federal or state emergency missions. I was one of those fulltime Army National Guard soldiers. My military title during this time frame was Warrant Officer - W01. Our federal organization mission during war time is to land artillery shells onto enemy forces, or in artillery soldier's terms, "putting steel on the target." A common scenario would be to provide artillery support to our Army infantry soldiers during combat. Each and every soldier in our organization was trained in their military occupation specialty -MOS to be part of the team to support the mission. That mission is to maintain properly trained and equipped units, available for prompt mobilization for war, national emergency, or as otherwise needed. Today the Army National Guard in conjunction with the Air National Guard, is a military force and a federal military reserve force of the United States. It partners with the Active Army and the Army Reserves in fulfilling our country's military when needed. During all of these middle Eastern conflicts within the last couple of decades in Iran, Iraq, and Afghanistan, the Army National Guard with their community soldiers, have been successful in performing their duties, while overseas defending our country, and making Americans live free.

This story is about one of those citizen soldiers who at the time held the rank of Private First Class – PFC Jimmy Gomez, his Military Occupational Specialty-MOS was 13A10 he trained as an Artillery Cannoneer at Fort Sill Oklahoma. Jimmy Gomez's primary job at the time was an ammunition handler. He and his team members inventoried, and issued live rounds of 105 Millimeter Artillery shells to each of the line Artillery Gun Batteries. When those shells were fired during training, it was his teams' job to pick up the empty shells or any remaining

live rounds and turn them into the Ammunition dump for inventory and security purposes.

Chapter 5

Street Fighter

Jimmy was born and raised in the tough streets of the South Bronx. He recently returned from Basic Combat Training–BCT, and Advanced Individual Training-AIT. A newly trained soldier by the United States Army; fresh out of BCT and AIT, no one knew anything about him. Being a young new soldier returning from BCT, and AIT, his new rank quickly became Private First Class. While in the Army National Guard Jimmy was responsible to attend one weekend a month of unit training, and two weeks during the summer months for annual training at Fort Drum. Watertown, NY.

Jimmy performed all his tasks well, it seemed that he takes his assignments, very serious and was task oriented. He accomplishes all his tasks as directed by his team leader. Jimmy showed very good character to his fellow

team soldiers, but he always seemed to be very cautious and skeptical to his fellow soldiers. It was not easy for Jimmy to allow people into his personal life. He also showed no interest in socializing with his fellow soldiers. He basically rolled with only those people that were business oriented, and gave no time to people who reported to duty that wanted to gossip about other soldiers. He pretty much held his own amongst his fellow soldiers both in skill level and his motivational level. He never spoke bad about anyone, and no one ever had anything bad to say about him. He shows no signs as being a quitter on any of his military assignments. Jimmy was always the first to report to duty and the last to leave. Because of the Army National Guard's commitment timetable, when there was no weekend duty or annual training duty, he spent most of his days back in the hood of the South Bronx. Knowing his economical living conditions and as a high school dropout, he fell into a common situation for youths living in this poverty district of the Bronx. Unemployment was also common during this decade, and most high school drop outs found it difficult to land a decent job. I was always concerned if Jimmy would be wise enough to keep away from the bad street gang members who try to recruit youths to join gangs to satisfy their financial needs. Youth gangs in general were involved with unlawful acts. Jimmy visited me at the armory occasionally during his non duty days, he often asked me if I needed any help. He wanted to make sure that I was aware, he was unemployed and available if there were additional duties for him going forward. I liked it when he showed up to help. I purposely began lining up tasks for him before he showed up during the week. I needed the help, and he could stay busy before he lands a fulltime job. I began to realize that his frequent visits helped him stay out of trouble, and helped me keep up with my workload. He began opening up about himself on his own, without me prying into his personal life. He was always looking for a civilian job, and I always reminded him to get his GED High School diploma first because he will have a better chance to find a job. I also reminded him, if you keep procrastinating you could find yourself taking the wrong path with the wrong people. He promised me, "that will never happen."

Gang violence was prevalent in the streets of the South Bronx. The number one reason is poverty. Many gangs existed mainly as a moneymaking enterprise. By committing thefts and dealing drugs gang members can make relatively large amounts of money. People who are faced with a lack of money may turn to crime if they can't earn enough with a legitimate job. Also, in Jimmy's case who lives in the heart of the neighborhoods with street gangs, he is up against peer pressure by the gang members. Gang members tend to recruit young people if they live in a gang dominated area.

Street gangs ruled their turf of the neighborhoods in the South Bronx, New York during the 1970's.

One day while I was working in the armory, I received a phone call from a New York City Police officer. The Police Officer said, "this is NYPD Police Officer Smith from the 41st Precinct anticrime unit. Is this Warrant Officer Ron

Sardanopoli?" I thought to myself, 41st Precinct (Fort apache) this is not going to be good news. The anticrime unit is a new program of undercover police officers that formed in 1970 it became a more effective way to fight crime. They are plain clothes men dressed to blend in with the neighborhood that they patrol. Their job is to prevent crime, and jump in to stop crime while it is happening. They have a very dangerous job. The 41st Precinct is one of the most violent precincts in New York City which is physically located in the South Bronx. In 1976 over eleven thousand serious crimes were reported by the 41st Precinct alone. One out of 15 people are victims of crime in their district. Over four thousand people were assaulted, robbed, raped or murdered the previous year in this district. "My response was, "Yes, how can I help you Officer Smith?" Officer Smith replied, "I'm getting ready to make multiple arrests because of gang members committing robbery. I have a Jimmy Gomez temporarily in my custody." My heart starts to palpitate, thinking, why would PFC Gomez be any part of street violence? P.O. Smith goes on to say, "Somehow Jimmy's story is shaping up to appear that he's a good guy, and I'm trying to verify his statement", I immediately, pulled the phone away from my mouth, and inhaled and exhaled a sigh of relief. P.O. Smith goes on to say, "Jimmy claims to be a member of the Army National Guard. I also want to verify his connection with the New York Army National Guard. Jimmy said that you can vouch for him." Smith was sounding like he was hoping that Jimmy was telling him the truth. I said, "Yes I can vouch for him." I began explaining to Police Officer Smith, "Jimmy Gomez is a citizen soldier who displays excellent character while attending military training with the New York Army National Guard. Jimmy's soldier skills and his positive team interaction with his team soldiers during missions is excellent. Since Jimmy enlisted into the New York Army National he has been a standup soldier." Police Officer Smith said, "great! That's all I needed to hear, his entire story checks out, I'll release him. There is just one other thing Mr. Sardanopoli, Jimmy Gomez was a hero today. A senior woman had her hand bag stolen and was roughed up by a bunch of very dangerous street gang members who are under arrest. Many adults who observed this assault did nothing to help this elderly woman. They fear the consequences that will happen to them by gang members if they interfere with their day to day acts of violence. Gomez didn't turn his head like the rest of the community members did. Jimmy Gomez witnessed this robbery, and began chasing the robbers on foot. As four gang members were fleeing the scene of the crime, one of them had the woman's hand bag. Gang members are usually successful when it comes to handbag snatching in these neighborhoods. This day was a bad day for these thugs who belong to a prominent and dangerous street gang." When Officer Smith mentions the name of the street gang, I could not help but to reflect on my knowledge about this specific gang via the local newspapers and TV. I heard so many bad things about this specific gang. I see their spray-painted artistry Logo name all around the streets, buildings and subway stations, in the territory that they control. This street gang started in the southern area of the Bronx, New York during the late 1960s, and gaining popularity in the 1970s. This gang was involved in a number of running battles with rival gangs. Officer Smith's voice tone and speech became dark, and feisty and said, "This time, one tough street kid by the name of Jimmy Gomez eye witnessed this woman's handbag ripped out of her hands, while gang members used physical violence which made her fall to the concrete sidewalk. Four young and desperate thugs ran and were not aware that this brave youth who has a heart of a lion, eye witnessed their criminal acts. Luckily, I so happen to be patrolling this neighborhood at the time. I was close by while this robbery was in progress. It was explained to me that a concerned citizen chased the robbers down the street. When I showed up at the scene, a fist fight was taking place. Jimmy Gomez against four gang member youths, these thugs were wearing gang vests with their Logo, and there was Jimmy Gomez in the middle of four gang members, I witnessed Jimmy dropping one of the two that was taller and about 50 pounds heavier than him. He was just finishing off his second robbery victim. One of the two victims that Jimmy laid out on the ground was still holding on to the senior woman's handbag. He solved the case for us, that was extremely dangerous and an honorable act by him. Jimmy is a very good street fighter. Don't let his size fool you, he packs a big punch. I suggest that somehow you convince him to take himself off the streets and to a New York City sanctioned Golden Gloves tournament gym. You will be helping him by taking his fists off the streets and into a youth center that has a boxing ring. Jimmy shows signs of having excellent, and very raw boxing skills. I'm telling you this because Jimmy speaks very highly of you, and told me that you're the only one he trusts. When I asked Jimmy to give me a family member name to call, he only trusted you to be his call for verification. Think about it, in many cases I have tried to help youths that show me that there is some good in them and take their fighting skills off the street and into the ring. If anything, the boxing gym would be a safe place for Jimmy to spend his time. Besides, once the word gets out to the street gang leader that Jimmy Gomez got four of their street gang members arrested, there is a good chance they will target him the next time they see him in or around their turf." P.O. Smith released Jimmy, and he is on his way over to the armory to talk to me about this incident.

This phone call by Police Officer Smith really put my thoughts in a tail spin. How can I dedicate or even manage the time to one soldier after duty hours, and at the same time be responsible to coordinate my time to my organizations mission? This temporary commitment may take away the time needed to function in my job. Maybe, if I just drop off Jimmy at a local gym and have a gym staff member take him under their wing? My thoughts were spinning in my head. Wait a minute; I need to talk to Jimmy about this whole idea. Who knows how he feels about Police Officer Smiths idea?

A couple of hours go by, I get a knock on my office door. I ask, "Who is it?" A voice responds, "Its Private First-Class Gomez Sir, request permission to enter." I said, “permission granted.” He came in and saluted, I saluted him back, its protocol. “Have a seat Private Gomez. First of all, are you ok?” Jimmy knew that I got P.O. Smiths phone call about the incident. Jimmy said, “yes, I’m ok, and thank you for vouching for me.” No problem Jimmy, “the truth will set you free.” Jimmy goes on to say, “just some lucky punches that found its way to my neck, but my knuckles are slightly cut and bruised, and he suddenly began cracking a slight smile.” It looked like he was proud and maybe appeared like he enjoyed his role in this fist fight. Jimmy continues, “and it’s not the first time I got into a street fight.” Jimmy explained, “I can’t stand gang members who are punks taking advantage of the senior people that live in my neighborhood. I get angry watching this happen in my neighborhood.” I told Jimmy, "You need to be careful messing with gang members.” Jimmy said, “I can’t help it, it was just instinct, it’s the gang members that were lucky the police showed up on time, not me." I told jimmy, "I am proud of you, for your bravery, you are worthy of some kind of citizen award. You need to find a more positive path to release this anger that street life gives you. Jimmy said, "first of all, I don't need any award for just protecting an elderly woman. If someone tried to give me an award to help a senior woman, I would never accept it."

I knew then, how special Jimmy was, for his humanitarian act, selfless character, and humble response. I'm thinking to myself, if there is just something, I could do for him that would make him find his way to a safer and positive future. At the same time provide him with support to stray him away from the demons that surround him in the streets of the South Bronx. Let me ask if he is interested in P.O. Smiths idea about training in a gym. Also, possibly entering the New York City Golden Gloves tournament."

I told Jimmy, "P.O. Smith was extremely impressed how you handled those thugs. He saw your fighting skills as you were fighting off these thieves'. He said that you pack a pretty good punch. Jimmy said, "If you don't know how to fight and you live in the streets of the hood, you will be beaten every day. I learned how to fight in the streets at a very young age." I asked, "So what do you think of stopping by a local gym that trains boxers for the Golden Gloves? We can go together, and find out more about it." Jimmy said, "Sure why not." I'm thinking, Jimmy might understand that getting into a boxing gym with the support of someone who believes in him might be his motivation to keep off the streets, and find more constructive things to do for himself. Besides, I always wanted to find some way that I could play a role into

helping someone that is stuck in the hood, find activities to lift his spirit and provide support.

Chapter 6

Morrisania Youth Center

I contacted the New York Daily News Golden Gloves department and asked if there was a gym in the South Bronx that trains boxers for the New York City Golden Gloves. They recommended the Morrisania Youth Center it is one of New York Daily News's Golden Gloves sanctioned gyms. The gym is located in the heart of the Morrisania section of the South Bronx. I said, "perfect, thank you." Well, that kind of worked out, the gym is located approximately ten New York City streets from my work place at the armory.

It was a very cold and windy winter night, this time of year with the clocks pushed back during the fall, the evenings came early, along with that so did the darkness. It was an eerie feeling, I didn't feel that it was safe to walk from my workplace to the gym, so the car ride to the

gym kept us warm and the burned down decayed buildings views were the same that I see when I travel to and from my workplace every day. More abandoned and decayed buildings, some were burned down to the ground. Homeless people hovering around a steel garbage pail filled with flammable pickings from the abandoned buildings used to build a fire to stay warm. The same weakened infrastructure was visible all over the South Bronx. Jimmy was my passenger on this ride, we both were looking at all this destruction and he never made a comment about it at all. As if that is the way of life for everyone, it becomes human nature for people to become a product of their environment. Jimmy just may know how to block these scenes out of his mind. In a sense Jimmy became part of the entire lifeblood of this community.

The way people are living continues to tear up my insides with grief and sadness.

When we got to the gym, the door was locked there were no signs on the door so we looked up and down the streets looking for someone that might know more about the hours of operation of this gym. All of a sudden in the distance we see a silhouette of a person walking briskly towards us. The few street lights that were working was able to give us a silhouette, of a youth carrying a gym bag. As he got closer to us, he stopped at the gym front door and was waiting with us. I was waiting for either Jimmy or this young fellow to strike a conversation. Neither one of them were even looking at each other. I said to myself, "I bet this is a street thing, one doesn't want to show each other their vulnerabilities." So, I asked this youth, what time does this gym open." He said, "Around 7pm, Chip opens the doors for us." So, does Chip own the gym? "No, he volunteers to coach the gym boxers, and he is also my boxing coach." I said, "My name is Ron, and we here to find out more about training a soldier from our organization to enter the Golden Gloves tournament." When I reached out to shake his hand, he tried to grab my thumb, for some sort of youth handshake; I immediately used my left hand to grab his to align my right hand for a traditional hand shake, and he immediately gave me a traditional hand shake. He said, "Hi, my name is Kenny" I was not very good at knowing the street handshakes at the time. When Jimmy introduced himself to Kenny, they synchronized perfectly in the most elaborate street hand shake. They locked thumbs, and grabbed each other's thumb with their entire right hand, and quickly switched into another hand shake. They curled the rest of their fingers on their shaking right hands and slid their hand away from each other into a 2nd hand shake. Their curled-up fingers locked into each other than shook their hands again in a up and down motion. Still holding each other's hand, and still staring each other into each other's eyes, not smiling, they both looked intense. After they performed their synchronized street hand shake, they both said to each other, 'Hey what's up man?" I was hoping that they would begin talking to each other, they just both stared on the ground immediately after the hand shake. I said to myself, "What just happened, am I behind times?" Jimmy came over to me and whispered, "Sir, if you're going to hang out with me on the streets, I have to teach you the street hand shake, that was not cool." I said, "Oh, so now I'm hanging out with you? We both got a good laugh out of that. As I turned around, coming from the opposite direction than Kenny did, I noticed a larger silhouette in the distance, Kenny said, "Here comes Chip" I said, "great we finally get inside, out from the cold" Kenny said, "It's just as cold inside as it is out here. The Youth Center doesn't have enough money to pay for the oil deliveries; someone donated an old used kerosene heater." I was wondering why the owner is not providing heat for the gym. Chip reaches the door and begins opening it for us, he said, who are the new faces?" Chip is an older man in his late sixties or early 70's. He is a big guy, guessing he boxed as a heavy weight in his day. I said, "Hi My name is Ron, and this is Jimmy Gomez who is one of our Army National Guard soldiers that would like to find out more about boxing, and possibly fighting in the Golden Gloves tournament." Chip said, "Hold on, has Jimmy ever boxed in a boxing ring before." Jimmy said, "No sir I haven't." Chip said, "ok your always invited to train in our gym. There is no fee; all coaches are volunteers with prior boxing experience. Our goal is to teach the sport of boxing to help the community kids, and in the same time it keeps them off the streets. I will watch over Jimmy, and coach you both in the game." I said, "Chip I'm not boxing I'm only here to support Jimmy." he said, "ok then, we don't have enough coaching volunteers, so you need to be here with Jimmy as his trainer, and I'll teach you how to coach/train your boxer. Talking to myself, "What have I just gotten myself into? My Job and family are not going to be happy to hear that working overtime in the streets of the South Bronx at night time to help a soldier get off the streets, I hope I could get everyone to understand." So, Chip went on to explain, "It's going to take about an hour for the gym to warm up with our Kerosene heater once we get it fired up." I was wondering to myself, "Are all gyms throughout New York City beat up like this one, with old equipment, taped up heavy bags, boxing ring posts were barely holding up the ropes, leaking roof with pails located in various parts of the gym to catch the dripping leaking water coming from the roof of the building. Even though it wasn't raining, they strategically located the pails in the same spots to catch the rain and melting snow leaking from the roof. Chip said, "everybody helps out here to keep the gym going." When pails fill up all boxers or trainers help out to empty the buckets. We don't have enough money to pay for the heating bill. After the kerosene heater warms up, the gym becomes packed. Chip said, "Let me show you the locker room" I'm thinking, the odor inside the gym wreaks body sweat, or something worse. The odor got worse as we entered the locker room. After about an hour goes by, and the gym begins to fill with youths, Jimmy and I along with Chip re-entered the locker room. Chip mumble some angry words to himself loud enough that we can hear, as he ran out to the center of the gym. He yelled, "Hey all you stinking, smelling (combined with some vulgar words) out here, I'm not your momma or your poppa, you all better learn to take home your stinking gym clothes and get them washed! the locker room smells like crap." After Chips rant, you could see that all boxers were respecting his wish, or maybe they heard it before. The response was more heartfelt and respected from the boxers, some responded, "yes daddy", followed by a good hardy laugh by most of them. There were boxers' sweats that were hanging in and out of the locker doors. I looked at the windows that were shut tight in the locker room and was wondering why not crack those windows to let in some fresh air. The windows were shut, especially during the winter months to retain the heat being generated by the portable kerosene heater. The smell of the burning kerosene did help camouflage some of the locker room smell. Still observing the terrible building conditions, and knowing that if this was a government or state building, Occupational Safety and Health Administration-OSHA would have closed it down for not meeting many safety codes. The ceiling was filled with large peeling paint chips, ready to fall from the ceiling. I realized now that this was probably an abandoned building that the community took for themselves and used it to help take the kids off the streets. This building will probably be a statistic soon as buildings are being torched every day. This gym is just another small sample size of how the under privileged youths made the best of their poverty-stricken lifestyle. Most of the building owners in the South Bronx stopped investing in repairs, as they seem to be waiting in line to torch, and get paid by the insurance companies. The boxers never complain about their surroundings, probably because they might think that this is how all the youth's centers are in New York City. This decayed South Bronx has affected these street kids. I expect a facility like this maybe in a third world country, not in this country.

Coach Chip is a very loyal and dedicated man, who also has a fulltime job; he dedicates his after-hour time towards community service. When he talks to any youth in this gym, they listen to him, more like a father figure. He provides them with trusting nurturing tough love when he is teaching the sport of boxing, and living the straight and narrow outside the gym. In my opinion, after knowing about the sport of boxing, Chip is one of the best corner men in the sport of boxing. Chip was a club fighter in his younger years. He also used the boxing ring as a way to escape the street fighting back in the 1920's. These kids who train here in this gym are all tough street kids that are trying to find a way to escape their current lifestyle in the streets of the South Bronx by taking their fists to the ring. Or maybe being the next boxing champion of the world.

Chip said to Jimmy, "ok let's warm up, jump rope until you hear the bell ring, stop when the bell rings, after a minute of rest the bell will ring again, start jumping rope. The bell is synchronized to the timing of a boxing round. When the bell rings everybody in the gym begins their 3-minute training. They train for 3 minutes continuously and they stop once the bell rings that constitutes one round. Rest for one minute, then after a minute the bell rings again, continue training for the next three minutes. Everybody in the gym follows this training timeline. The training stations are jumping rope for a warm up, stretching to limber up to avoid injury. Shadow boxing in front of large mirrors to help develop more powerful and accurate punches, it helps in developing the body and hand power plus speed to synchronize into the perfect body or head blow. Abs workout to strengthen the stomach, the abs are always tested in a boxing match, many boxers have lost fights due to showing up with weak abs. Punching the heavy bag with boxing gloves to develop power, and punching technique, the speed bag to develop punching rhythm, and speed. The final workout station is three rounds of boxing against someone that is in your weight class or close to it. After Jimmy finished his jump rope station for his warm up, and finished stretching, he began shadow boxing. Chip stopped Jimmy and began teaching him foot and body positioning when throwing a punch. I noticed Jimmy giving me looks through the mirror that he was beginning to tire, he kind of smiled about it. Chip noticed his long face smiling and said don't look around for sympathy, you have a lot more stations you need to get done tonight. Let's see how tough you really are? Jimmy wiped off the smile on his face and began digging into his workouts.

As Jimmy was going through his stations, I noticed a middle age man walking into the gym, and he had a young boxer behind him. The entire gym all focused on both guys and his boxer. They both seem well respected by all.

As this middle-aged fellow walked in, he immediately locked his eyes on me while walking up to Chip. It seems that he wanted to know who I was. I could see across the gym as Chip was explaining who we were they both were looking my way. It looks like he wanted to find out who I was and why I was here. All of a sudden, this large muscular wide frame guy began walking in my direction and a young amateur boxer with boxing gloves laced over his neck who came in with him began walking into the locker room to change into his sweats for training. He continued walking in my direction and when he reached me, he came across with very welcoming gestures a large smile and put out his right hand with a traditional hand shake, I shook his hand. His arms and the size of his hands were huge, it felt like his fingers covered the back of my hand. He said, "My name is Leon Washington, and I have been providing community service to the Morrisania gym since 1974." I said, "Hi Leon my name is Ron Sardanopoli, I am stationed at the Franklin Avenue Armory on 168th street, a few of blocks from here. Leon said, "I know that armory and neighborhood, the amateur boxer Davie Moore that I train is from 168th Street. I'm with the Army National Guard and trying to help a soldier find a better path from the streets to the gym. Leon said, "first of all do you mind if I call you Mr. Ron? because I'll never remember that last name. I said, "Yes Ron is fine" Leon said, "Ron you came to the right place. I came from the streets of the South Bronx myself. All I did was street fighting; I was living on the wrong sides of the tracks during my younger days. If it wasn't for good supportive people like yourself suggesting I take my fists to the gym, I may have ended up in jail or dead. After my amateur years, I turned professional, and retired as a professional boxer in 1974. I have been volunteering my service to help train amateur boxers ever since I retired as a professional boxer." Well I guess my boxer Jimmy and I are in the right place. I'm trying to help Jimmy find a more productive path away from hanging around the streets while he is not conducting military duties. A 41st Precinct New York police officer saw him in a street fight against gang members. According to the police officer, Jimmy laid out two of his attackers as he was helping a senior woman who was a victim of a handbag robbery. The police officer recommended that I consider taking him to the gym to perfect his skills, if anything it will keep him out of trouble. Leon said to me, "take a look around this entire gym Ron. Everyone is here for the same reason. Some of these boxers have already been in and out of jail. They are all looking for a chance to become the next boxing champion, and maybe land a big jackpot, cash contract to box one day. It really all melts down to, keeping them off the streets." I can see now why these amateur boxers are so motivated, they believe they can be the next champ.

When Leon walks into the gym. Leon attracts everyone attention for his boxing knowledge and his strict gym rules and guide lines. No one really wants to get on his bad side, he genuinely wants every amateur boxer to succeed and exceed their potential, at the same time he treats every amateur boxer hardcore. If they are not here to train, you're wasting Leon's time. I could see it in his eyes when he speaks to them. He wanted me to make sure; while I was there training Jimmy that I understand his position in his community service. I often thought how successful Leon would be if he would join the Army and become a drill sergeant and train new recruits during the basic training phase. Soldiers need a focused dedicated leader like Leon Washington to toughen up our young soldiers and teaching them to be independent. While Leon was talking to me, he was also scanning all the amateur boxers, making sure they were executing their punches properly. He noticed Jimmy was up to shadow boxing in front of this very large mirror where five boxers were alongside Jimmy and each other to shadow box. Leon yelled, "Hey Jimmy that's not how you throw a right-hand punch" Leon showed jimmy how to position his feet when throwing his punches to gain his maximum power into the punch, and the speed to quickly return his hands to a defensive position to block his opponent punches. Leon tells Jimmy, "Now I want you to repeat that punch, until it sinks in and becomes your own right-hand punch." Then Leon said to me, "Ron, listen and learn. There will be times through the Golden Gloves tournament that Chip or I will be matched up with other amateur boxers at different event locations, and you will be alone with Jimmy in his corner as his trainer/coach. Jimmy will need you to provide fighting instructions and first aid for nose bleeds or cuts when needed. We will show you how this is all done" I said, "I'm all ears, thanks." With that Leon went around the gym, with his very serious demeanor and began helping all the amateur boxers. His corrections were loud enough that everyone in the gym could hear. Leon yells, "Hey Kenny, when you throw that left hook, do it in way, imagine swatting a bee in front of your face, and try adding a right cross to that combination." To another boxer he yelled, "hey, when you're backing up and throwing counter punches, make sure your back foot is planted to develop more power." Leon began showing the boxer his boxing form and moves, how to step back, while counter punching. Leon has high spirit and motivation for the youths in the gym. Leon also puts time into policing up boxers who exercise their jaws instead of their body, Leon yells out, "listen up yawl, your all here to train, not talk about how your day has been or some bulls**t. This is not a social club hangout, your only here to work, train and learn. Remember this, when you walk into that ring against your opponent your all alone, and nothing is guaranteed. It's up to you whether you want to be a winner or a loser. When you come to this gym train hard, don't waste my time or your time."

I stood by Jimmy, and watched him on the heavy bag; Chip came over to help him as Jimmy was showing signs of exhaustion. Jimmy said my arms feel like heavy weights, I hardly can hold them up", Chip said "this is your first day of training, like all new boxers, you are out of shape, it's going to take many days and weeks of training to develop the strength and endurance, and skill to box three rounds against a trained boxing opponents. In your last training station, I want you to box three, three-minute rounds with someone in your weight class. Jimmy, we will hold off on sparring for tonight. After you're done with the heavy bag, get your time in for the speed bag and I'll show you how the punching timing is done on the speed bag, and end off on working your abs. A boxer's abs workout is more intense than the basic sit-up exercise. You will sleep well tonight." Chip told me, "make sure Jimmy does road work every day, and make it to the gym Monday, Wednesday, and Friday nights. Jimmy is carrying too much excess body weight, his training will get him down to a lighter weight, which will be his fighting weight. Eat portion size meat, eggs, tuna, peanut butter, and milk are an excellent source of protein. Remember, this is boxing and not weightlifting. You need to be lean and mean. Lots of fruits and vegetables, everybody needs vitamins, this is a requirement to be a healthy person in general. Eat a wide variety of them. Plenty of Water, water, water! One gallon a day is a minimum for everybody in general. Two to three gallons is a must if you work out hard. Again, this is a minimum, if you can drink more, do it. Stay away from alcohol, it will slow you down and at the same time fatten you up. In regards to Jimmy's body fat, this has more to do with his genetic makeup than anything. If you have a body that builds up fat easily, stay away from unhealthy fats for at least five days out of the week. It's ok to enjoy your food once a week since boxing training is very tough and will burn off the fat quickly, anyways no ice cream or candy, and no fried foods."

After the work out Jimmy was exhausted, it was late and Jimmy said that he will walk home from here. I said to Jimmy, "everything is happening so quickly, lets slow it down. Let's just talk about what you and I are agreeing on. If you want me to be your handler during your training for the Golden Gloves tournament, I want to see you improve your life overall. You currently are unemployed, and you dropped out of high school. You already know that how jobs are scarce and not available to high school dropouts, and the youths that get jobs have a high school diploma. So, this is what I'm asking you to do if you want me in your corner. First get into night school to get your GED diploma, once you get your GED, this will help you land a secure fulltime job. One day you will be able to afford your own housing. Jimmy said, "first thing tomorrow I will sign up for a GED program" We shook hands, first the traditional hand shake, then Jimmy said, wait now let me show you the street shake, so we did it and got another good chuckle out of it. I told Jimmy, "I could give you a ride to where ever you want to go." He said, "he wanted to be alone and think about managing his time to box and getting his GED. OK, let me know if you want to move forward with this, give me a call or drop by my office tomorrow. Thinking to myself," there are only three kinds of people that use the streets of the South Bronx at night time, policemen, criminals and potential victims. Jimmy knows the streets, and he could handle himself if he needs to. I'm sure he knows his way around the neighborhoods. I asked him again, "I could drop you off at a train station, or a bus stop." He laughed and said, "No thank you."

Chapter 7

Missing

A couple of days go by and there is no word from Jimmy, he missed his next training day at the gym. I thought then, that he decided not to enter the tournament. Maybe he got himself a fulltime job and found a way to keep off the streets and out of trouble. I hope I'm not being too optimistic, because I can't stop thinking that he is in some kind of danger. Maybe I should have tried harder to give him a ride to a bus stop or train station after his last gym workout. If he decided not to enter the tournament, I am not scheduled to see him until his next military weekend training duty.

One entire week goes by and I got a phone call from New York Police Officer Smith from the 41st Precinct. P.O. Smith said, "Hello Mr. Sardanopoli this is P.O. Smith, while working last night there was a gang related gathering around the same area where Jimmy had his battle with gang members, it made me think about Jimmy Gomez, how is he doing?" I responded, "I'm a bit concerned, I took your advice and help convince him to go to the Morrisania Youth Center for some boxing training, and he did, and did very well. The gym has a couple of experienced volunteer coaches that showed interest in working with Jimmy as long as I was there with him as his coach. At the end of his first training night, we left the gym, it was dark, the few street lights that were working barely gave enough light, especially along the darker side streets. I offered Jimmy a ride and he wanted to walk home alone instead." P.O. Smith asked, "do you know where he lives." That is a good question; "Jimmy never discussed where he lives or who he lives with." P.O. Smith asked, "Could he be homeless?" I'm thinking, "I never even thought that was his situation. Well right now I have not seen him for an entire week, and he is scheduled to attend his next scheduled military meeting with the Army National Guard in a week." P.O. Smith said, "I have street contacts in the neighborhood that I patrol, I'll ask around." Thanks, "give me a number where I can reach you, if he shows up in our training weekend, I'll let you know." I'll call you." P.O. Smith said, "I rather not, being undercover, I'll call you back in a couple of weeks, and don't worry about Jimmy, he probably has a good reason not showing up to his gym workouts." "ok, thanks talk to you soon."

Now I'm really concerned, let me check with my headquarters, and ask them to check on his personal records for a home of or telephone number on file. So, the headquarters representative called Jimmy's home number on file, and a recording came on saying, "Temporary out of order or disconnected." I checked on Jimmy's home address on the emergency alert list on file, and decided to drive by that address on my way home. The address that Jimmy had on file led me to a building that was burned by a fire. It looked like it was part of a larger fire, as many buildings on this street were burned and demolished. Buildings stayed decayed and burned for many years during this timeframe in the South Bronx, it was difficult to know when this building actually burned down to the ground. Many soldiers that trained with our Army National Guard organization that lived in the South Bronx were affected by these living conditions. Jimmy is just another soldier trying to survive during this unfortunate poverty era, trying to make something out of his life, without healthy living conditions, and a family support system, there was so much anxiety and stress for the families, and youths during this decade.

Let me try driving by the Morrisania gym, and see if Jimmy was seen at the gym recently. The gym was just opening up, and Chip was there and asked, "What happened to Jimmy Gomez?" I said, "That's why I'm here Chip, I have not heard from him since the one night that he started training here, and I'm concerned." Chip said, "I wouldn't worry so much about Jimmy Gomez's desire to box, mainly because when I teach him, he has a good understanding of the sport, and he is a fast learner, I see it in his eyes he is all in. Once these amateur boxers who train here get back out on the streets, they very easily get their heads redirected with their street life, but I see something different in Jimmy. Give him some time; I think you will see him return to the gym soon." I said, "I hope so Chip, the Golden Gloves tournament is coming up soon, and he has not even learned the fundamentals of the sport. Chip said, "I'll let you know if Jimmy can handle himself in the upcoming tournament, I have a very good fighter by the name of Kenny Mitchell who is in his weight class that Jimmy can spar." I said, "Yes Kenny, I met him the first day; he did mention that you were his coach." Chip said, "I'm everybody's coach, when I see that some fighters like Kenny have what it takes, having the heart and boxing skills to improve, and makes it to the gym every night, I tend to work with them more than the others. Kenny Mitchell is one of those fighters, he will be entering the Golden Gloves tournament this year as well." OK, Chip, thanks for your vote of confidence, I'll stop looking for Jimmy, and let him find himself." Chip said, "Ron leave me your phone number, if Jimmy stops by the gym, I'll have him call you, or I'll call you." "Will do Chip, I'll leave my office number, thanks."

I left that gym saying the words Chip wanted to hear from me. In reality, I'm not a product of the streets of the

South Bronx like Chip was. I really cannot make the connection of Jimmy figuring it out on his own, while hanging out in the streets owned by gang members. I know that Chip, and Leon were both products of being street fighters in the South Bronx who found their way off the streets via the boxing gym. After hearing from Police Officer Smith concerning Jimmy's where a bouts, and driving by Jimmy's home of record on file to find a burned down building. I am more concerned about Jimmy's safety than ever before.

Jimmy did say to me at the end of the night after his gym workout, "I wanted to be alone and think about actually putting in the time to box." So, I'll take Chip's advice and let Jimmy figure out his own life, and make his own decisions. I'm still concerned, hopefully he is safe.

It's finally here our military training weekend Saturday morning, I'm in my office, an hour before our next Army training weekend formation. Preparing our soldiers for their Saturday morning formation. The uniform of the day was their fatigue olive drab uniform with their baseball soft cap, to include the proper name tag and insignia patches sewed to comply with regulation, to include their ranks. Their trousers need to be bloused above their polished combat boots. All soldiers had to wear their pistol belt to make sure that all required attachments to their belt were available in case these soldiers got the call to mobilize for federal or state duty. The attachments to their pistol belt at that time were two ammo pouches to store their caliber 7.62 ammunition rounds, for their M14 Rifle. A first aid pouch that stored their first aid kit, and in the rear of the pistol belt was their very neatly tighten poncho held on with bungee cords. The field shoulder straps that were attached to the pistol belt to help holdup any additional equipment loads needed for their mission.

Once the soldier's uniform and equipment belt were squared away. The soldier headed to the weapons room, where after presenting their weapons card to their supply sergeant they were issued their personal M-14 rifle. Immediately after they were issued their weapon, they headed to this large drill floor which is the size of a football field for formation and inspection for clothing and arms.

They called Artillery subunits Battery, and they call Infantry Subunits Company. Being assigned at this armory to an Artillery Battalion the proper title for our units are called, Battery. There was a total of five Battery's that made up this Artillery Battalion, each has their own title to distinguish one from the other, as each distinguished Battery also had their own specific duties to accomplish their mission that we are assigned. For Instance, our Headquarters Battery provided administrative, leadership and staff support. The 105MM

Artillery Gun Batteries A, B, and C, their job is to land artillery shells on their targets, each gun battery has soldiers that are qualified cannoneers and are skilled to operate and fire these guns. They are comprised of teams of qualified soldiers, who fire 105MM Artillery shells using a 105 Howitzer tow weapon. The last of the five Battery's is the Service Battery which was the unit that helped maintain the cannons for the 3-gun Batteries. They also drove trucks that hauled the ammunition for the Artillery pieces.

All of a sudden while viewing all the soldiers in the Battalion lining up into formation by the command, A commander's order "Dress right dress" soldiers measure off each other to be aligned in a perfect distance for inspection. My eyes immediately caught one soldier, Private First-Class Jimmy Gomez. I felt rejoiced that very moment while setting eyes on him. He looked squared away, like a model soldier, his uniform was starched, boots shining, and proper haircut. As the work day went by, I gave Jimmy no extra attention, like nothing ever happened to him. At this point, I thought that Jimmy decided not to pursue the idea of taking his fists to the ring, and to learn the sport of boxing. I was ok with it if that was his decision. I was just only at this point, very happy that he was safe, and back on track conducting his military obligation.

After final formation that ended the duty day, there is a knock on my door. I ask who it is, he said, “Its Private First-Class Jimmy Gomez request permission to enter sir.” I said, “Please do PFC Gomez, and have a seat.” Jimmy began the conversation and said, “I appreciate your support for me, with your efforts to help me. Working after duty hours with me at the Morrisania gym. I don’t want to be taking on this boxing venture without you.” I jokingly said, “Hold on it’s a onetime elimination tournament, which means, the first fight you lose it becomes a very short journey for me and you.” We both laughed. Jimmy immediately responded, “Tell your family your time from your family will last the entire tournament because I don’t plan on losing.” I said, “now you sound like a winner.” Jimmy wanted me to know that he has not missed a step in pursuing his personal boxing training. He explained, “I could not make it to the gym, because I was helping my brother move to a new apartment with his wife and children, and now I’m living with them temporarily. “Here is my new address for my personnel file record.” I took a quick glance at the street, and I immediately recognized the street name and its location. He is living away from the high crime area of the South Bronx. He also went on to say, “I have been running morning and nights every day for a week, and shadow boxing, practicing different combinations of left jabs, right cross, and left hooks. I'm eating better, no fried foods, or cake and candy. I feel like I lost some weight." I didn't want to tell Jimmy about any of the follow-up I was doing to try to find him for the last two weeks. I wanted Jimmy to figure it out all on his own, which he did. I said, "ok Private Gomez, I will see you 7pm tomorrow evening at the gym for your next training day. I remember Chip saying that after your warm up, he was going to observe you sparring three, three-minute rounds with someone in your weight class." Jimmy said, "Yes he did say that, bring him on I'm ready to fight."

The next morning after the weekend drill I received a phone call from Police Officer Smith. He wanted to know if Jimmy Gomez showed up for his military formation this past weekend? I said, "Jimmy was present and accounted for" he asked, "What happened?" I explained, "He had to help his brother and his family move, and Jimmy is now living with his brother." P.O. Smith said, "Well now at least you know he is not homeless." "Yes" I agreed." P.O. Smith said, "I'll follow Jimmy's Golden Glove tournament matches in the Daily Newspaper," P.O. Smith put many youths into the Police Athletic League gym to enter the Golden Gloves tournament, helping them to get them off the streets and into a more productive environment. P.O. Smith said, "I'm glad this is working out for Jimmy. "

Chapter 8

Up for the challenge

I give Jimmy a lot of credit to man up tonight. Jimmy is going to spar against another boxer that probably has the same background story line as he does. Jimmy just found out that he will be sparring against Kenny Mitchell. Kenny has been coming to the Morrisania boxing gym since he was fourteen years old. Chip has been Kenny's trainer, and I know Kenny can box, I saw him sparring the first day I arrived to the gym. It takes a certain type of person that is willing to step into a ring to get his head beat on. Some of the best professional fighters come from urban areas; they survived the urban streets either with their fists, some will use whatever means to survive. They pretty much face danger more often than the average youths, there is always this unknown fear of getting in the ring with an experienced amateur boxer for the first time. I

know Jimmy is nervous tonight, his face turning colors, his breathing is already heavy, and he didn't even start his warm up drills. I said to Jimmy, "ok Jimmy let's begin jumping rope until you perspire to get warmed up." Jimmy was not a person who communicated his thoughts or feelings. He was always about being a good listener to the people he trusts and pretty much takes care of business even when the odds are against him, whether he is boxing or performing military training missions. While Jimmy was jumping rope, I reviewed his many combinations with him, "left jab, right cross, right uppercut, left hook, and make sure your legs and feet are planted to get the most power out of each punch. Always have your hands up protecting your chin, and deliver all your punches from your chin and quickly return to your chin to defend yourself from counter punches. Always protecting your chin and head." Chip walked over to us and said to Jimmy, “welcome back we thought you gave up on the idea to learn the sport of boxing.” Jimmy said, “I never quit, I just had to take care of my personal stuff. I was looking for a new place to live, and I never stopped training on my own and dieting. I ran every morning and evening.” Chip said, “let’s see how you do tonight, I have you set to spar with Kenny” I was glad to hear Chip tell Jimmy that Kenny is on a higher level when it comes to boxing skills. Kenny has already competed in local gym boxing tournaments. Kenny is one of the better boxers that is in Jimmy’s weight division. He will be a good test for Jimmy. Jimmy completed having his hands wrapped with gauze to protect his knuckles and bones on both hands.

I noticed Leon Washington just coming into the gym, with the same amateur boxer that he did the last time I was here. Leon walked over to Chip to get an update of what the game plan was for all the boxers. Immediately after talking with Chip to get his update, he walked straight over to me. Leon greeted me, and said, "So tonight is Jimmy's first spar session. Kenny will give Jimmy a good spar session, they both are carrying the same weight, I'll be watching."

I ask Leon, "By the way who is that boxer that comes in with you?" Leon said, "His name is Davie Moore, he came into the gym last year, and told me that he will be the best boxer in this gym in one year. Davie lied; he became the best boxer in the gym in three months. After three months Davie became the New York Daily News 1976 Welter Weight Golden Gloves Champion. So, Davie built up his confidents, coming from the streets of the South Bronx and winning his first Golden Gloves Championship in three months. When Davie came out of the locker room, Leon called Davie over and introduced Davie to

Jimmy and I. Davie spoke so softly, and came across extremely respectable. I didn't hear any street language or toughness in his voice. Leon said to us, "Davie came off the streets and into this gym like you did Jimmy, and the rest is history. Three months later Davie became a Welterweight Golden Gloves Champion." It takes hard work, commitment, and heart. Jimmy also included, "Corazon", Jimmy's nationality is Puerto Rican so he translated Leon's word, the word heart in his Latino language, is pronounced "Corazon." Jimmy went on to say, that is his street nickname, because I don't fear anyone. That was the first sign of seeing and hearing another side of Jimmy. I'm starting to hear and see motions and sounds of Jimmy's street personality. The parts that he holds back during his military training with the Army National Guard. Leon is very familiar with the Latino word, Corazon, because he has worked in the corner with many Latino amateur boxers in the past and present. Leon yelled out, "ok next up is Kenny Mitchell vs. Jimmy Gomez."

I jumped up in the corner of the ring platform outside the ropes, and I used my knee and my hands to spread open the ropes to allow Jimmy to enter the ring. I have his water bottle, towel, and bucket. Chip was stationed in the other corner with Kenny. I checked Jimmy's gloves and head gear to make sure they were snug. I placed a light coat of Vaseline on his face. We already have a bell ringing pattern that runs through the entire gym. The bell is on its one-minute rest period, Chip yells across the ring, "as soon as the next bell rings, start boxing." I put water on Jimmy's mouth piece, and place it in his mouth. Jimmy and Kenny waiting for the bell to ring. They begin their boxing rhythm styles by jumping in place, and shadow boxing to stay warm before the bell rings. The bell rings and they get closer to each other towards the center of the ring. Kenny begins his punching combinations as he begins getting his routine ring workout in. Kenny immediately delivers two crisp straight left-hand jabs to Jimmy's face, then a left hook to his ribs. Jimmy backed up, and seemed surprised, shocked, by Kenny's hard and crisp combinations. Kenny noticed Jimmy not throwing punches in return, only trying to block his punches. Kenny continued to follow Jimmy to the ropes not giving him enough time to counter punch, or begin delivering his offensive combinations. I yelled out, "Jimmy let your hands go, counter punch!" his only reaction was to hold up his fists by his face and not move around, just trying to block Kenny's punches. I yelled out, "Jimmy step to the side and counter punch, get off the ropes." He was frozen with his back against the ropes, somehow not knowing how to get out of his situation. Leon noticed Jimmy pinned against the ropes, and he yelled out, "now Jimmy you're here to work, not being a punching bag, so jab him." Jimmy begins to jab Kenny, with Kenny's boxing experience he was able to block his jabs and Kenny counter punch Jimmy's first left jab by delivering a very fast and hard right crosses over Jimmy's left jab, and followed with a left hook. That counter punch hit Jimmy on the left side of his jaw and wobbled him, and you can see Jimmy's legs wobble. I began thinking, "maybe this is not such a good idea to help guide him to a boxing ring." I don't see any signs of that tough guy, who supposedly is a very good street fighter, according to Patrolman Smith. This went on for three minutes; Jimmy could not get a punch in. When the bell rang to end round one. Jimmy came to the corner, and said, "my face hurts." I said, "Kenny knows that you are not going to punch back, and he is dominating the situation." I noticed Jimmy face slightly red where Kenny delivered the blow. Do you want me to stop the fight? Jimmy said, "hell no." I raised my voice to energize his tempo, "then get in there and take the lead, throw the first punch, show him why you came here. Continue to keep your hands up" Jimmy nodding his head with confidence, understanding what he has to do. I liked that he showed no sign of fear. I said, "Jimmy let your hands go, keep punching, Leon said, "Jimmy as you back into the ropes, keep jabbing, and use your left hand to turn him, and deliver left hooks to the body." The bell rings for the 2nd round, and Jimmy runs into Kenny's corner and begins throwing wild punches some were effective, nothing that he learned in the gym, it almost appeared to look like punches thrown in a street fight, but more accurate to his target. His punches were so fast and powerful. Kenny didn't know how to react to his punches, so he backed away using his excellent foot work. Jimmy prowled Kenny and would not let him leave his punching distance. Jimmy's punches were like an automatic weapon, one after another, left, right, left, right. Kenny's rhythm was thrown off, he did not have enough time to counter Jimmy's punches and now Kenny is holding his fists up to protect his jaw. Jimmy was delivering non-stop over hand lefts and rights. He continued to deliver punches one after the other, non-stop, hard thrown punches, like a machine gun. Kenny blocked some of them, not all the punches, Jimmy's punches were so fast and powerful that some punches went through Kenny's defense and landed on his chin. The bell rings to end the 2nd round. Leon was with me observing Jimmy in this 2nd round and said, "Ron you have a good fighter on your hands, he is strong for his size. He just needs to learn technical boxing skills, but he has what it takes to be a good fighter. Make sure he keeps coming back to the gym." I now witnessed what Police Officer Smith observed when he witnessed Jimmy fighting in the streets of the South Bronx. Jimmy is a tough kid and he fights with non-stop rage, like nothing you ever saw before. I'm beginning to make a connection that the youths of the South Bronx are tough street kids because they are products of their tough environment. To be able to survive during this horrific decade gave them empowering cognitive and physical power and strength to withstand many obstacles that come their way. When Jimmy returned to his corner, Leon told him, "much better Jimmy, now the only thing you need to learn is the sport of boxing, sizing up your opponent, and learning how to protect yourself, and putting together combinations," Chip said, "two rounds is enough for Jimmy on his first night sparring, make sure Jimmy finishes the rest of his training stations tonight, heavy bag, speed bag, abs workout, etc." I sensed that Jimmy had a feeling of accomplishment after showing me and the gym coaches how tough he really is. Kenny walked over to Jimmy after their sparring session and told him, "you will be a good fighter, just keep coming back to the gym to train." That was a sign of great sportsmanship by Kenny.

Jimmy had a great feeling coming out of this training session. He was glowing, with a big crooked smile, the crooked smile was supported with some black and blue swelling, while he was smiling, I iced the side of his face that showed redness and slight swelling that came from Kenny's heavy punches during the 1st round of this sparring session. I knew now that Jimmy could fight, and I am all in to help him transform and mold his street fighting skills into a successful amateur boxer. I also want Jimmy to learn more about his life during this journey. I'm beginning to vision a successful development in him, not only to be a better boxer, but to be a standup citizen with an education and a job. The difference at this point in his development is he doesn't have to fight in the streets to let out his anger and end up getting in trouble. He could take his fists to the gym and use boxing gloves and head gear for his safety, and let his boxing skills create change in his life. At the end of the day he and his gym opponents are friends not enemies, and Jimmy develops camaraderie with his gym stable mates who were once street fighters also. Boxing is a real change model, watching street youths using the gym, day in and day out to help build self-esteem, caring, maturity, and integrity for themselves. These lessons cannot be taught in the streets of the South Bronx.

Chapter 9

Training to Hip Hop

After listening to several trainers to include Chip and Leon, who are retired professional boxers, and observing and studying my day to day gym experience. I put together my own notes and drew out a training plan that will prepare Jimmy to fight at the amateur level. This is what I learned, and shared with Jimmy, "I put together the very minimum of what you should be able to do all in one day. if you want to compete at the amateur level you need run three to five miles without getting to tired. Jump rope for 30 minutes straight, throw combinations and hit the heavy bag with power punches for 15 minutes non-stop. Spar with any amateur from any gym, and do as many sit-ups as you can. End your workout with pushups, as many that you can do. By accomplishing this

training every day with an occasional rest day, this means that you have the stamina and conditioning to compete at the amateur fight-level. If you can do them all, then you're in pretty good shape and conditioned to compete." This is what Jimmy needed to accomplish to get into shape to fight in the New York Daily News Golden Gloves Tournament. I also told Jimmy, "have fun and test yourself on the physical benchmarks that I laid out for you. As you progress in your training, make sure you are not too hard on yourself if you can't hit any benchmark, because eventually you will."

Being an amateur boxer is extremely physically demanding. Competitive fighting doesn't purely judge on skillful execution or who "fought better." It is simply a contest of points, which are scored by direct hits. Quite often, a boxing competition can resemble an awkward game of tag more so than a boxing movie. On the other hand, amateur boxing can also become bouts of pure aggression. You can be as skillful as you want, but if you're only throwing 40 punches a round and your opponent throws 225, it makes a hard case for judges to give you the fight. I've been observing Jimmy's spar session and he is more like the opponent that throws 225 punches nonstop.

During my work day, Jimmy would pass by the armory to square away his military locker, inventory and align his uniforms. He also checks in with me to see if I need any help. This is when he updates me on his training, I.e. his long training runs, sit-ups, and pushup amounts, and chats about his boxing training schedule and his diet. I began seeing the distribution of his bodyweight trim down, and his arm and chest muscles were developing by showing athletic definition. I continued to impound in him the understanding that meeting all his training goals will make him a very good boxing opponent for any amateur boxer in his weight class. Whether it's a lot of running or punching, you need to be prepared to do lots of both. Yes, skill is more important than power and endurance but only when you have reached the minimum levels of conditioning for boxing will you then be capable of applying your skills to fights. Your boxing skill developments will come while training at the gym, by observing the experience fighters, and taking on better fighters to spar. Jimmy responded by completely understanding the tools of boxing, and knows his capabilities. It seems the training weeks are now flying by. Jimmy's private life is still very private to him, but at least now his street time was transferred to his boxing training at the gym. I never let go of my thoughts, thinking about the current poverty level that surrounds him and people that live in these communities. The evening driving to Jimmy's address on record to find his building and the buildings around him were burnt *to the* ground left a crushing memory in me. I never tried prying into his personal life, but I have to gain some knowledge to help me help him get through his future day to day training, and of course his personal life. I asked Jimmy, "you have become a skilled boxer in such a short period of time, you learned so quickly, and your demeanor when fighting is excellent for the ring. I only know of your one street fight from the New York Police Officer that brought us together. How many street fights have you had where you fought others for whatever reason? Was it five times, or 15 times?" Jimmy immediately flashes a cynical smile, and asked, "are you serious?" He was referring to those numbers I suggested. "It's more like hundreds," he said. I knew him by now, and he was being very honest with me. He now made me realize that his street fighting experience is going to mean a lot as he moves forward in this boxing tournament. So, his combined fighting experience is not only associated to the three months' time he spent at the gym, but also those street fights that he has fought while fighting those demons associated with the lifeblood of the hood.

At this point Jimmy is very well-trained, he is anxious to get into the ring with his first Golden Gloves opponent. Jimmy really likes his training regiment, and what he likes most is to see his opponents flat on the mat. I'm constantly observing the many training activities around the gym. The fighters variously skip rope, hit the bag, do jumping knee-lifts, bob their heads up and down to simulated avoiding getting punched in the head. This is all in synchrony with the tunes of the popular Hip-Hop music that was found in the 1970's by artists who were raised in the South Bronx. Suddenly the Hip-Hop song stops mid-stream and we all focus on a boxer lying flat on his back with his boom box by his side. Everyone's eyes zoomed in on a boom box, and we realized that he shut off his hip-hop music coming out of his boom box. He just finished up his workout and began carrying his boom box on his shoulder heading out the door, he and four other boxers leave the gym.

Before I go on, let me pause this segment for the readers to explain, what a boom box is. The boom box is an oversized radio that played music stations, and cassette tapes, usually carried on a youth's shoulders, it was a large and heavy radio. They were built with a very powerful power amp. In this case the boom box was so large and powerful and the sound filled an entire gym with very loud hip-hop music for everyone to hear. The boom box quickly became associated with urban society, particularly Black and Hispanic youths. With the new Hip-Hop culture being blasted across the urban streets during the 1970's, combined with new media invention called the boom-box, it seemed that every youth in the South Bronx owned a boom-box. A lot of citizen complaints about the very loud music being blasted on city streets, public parks, and public transportation in buses and trains became a disturbance. The complaining citizens nicked named the boom box, "ghetto blasters", as a backlash to express their disbelief that the youths of our society were allowed to carry this type of radio device in the public.

As four boxers proceeded to leave the gym with their boom box, the gym quieted down, you can hear a pin drop. A disbelief while hearing their footsteps of those boxers dissolving while heading to the front door, and then the sound of the squeaking front door slammed closed. All the gym boxers slowed down their workout activities, almost not feeling the rhythm of the hip-hop music to help them train. Now it seemed that all their thoughts are synchronizing with the realization that their rhythm to the Hip-Hop music is gone. Wondering how they all are going to get their training rhythm back without the beat of Hip-Hop playing in the back ground. Suddenly another boxer runs into the locker room and runs back out into the gym area with his boom box. Once the hip-hop bogey beat music was raised for everyone to hear, the boxers all began training again to the rhythm of the music. Many boxers showed appreciation to the boxer that shared his boom box. The boxers all seem to feel upbeat to train to the backdrop rhythm of the Hip-Hop beat.

One reason that Hip-Hop music is very special to the youths of the South Bronx is because the Hip-Hop movement started in the South Bronx. During the 1970's the urban movement known as "Hip-Hop" began to develop in the South Bronx area of New York City focusing on emceeing, breakbeats, and house parties. Starting at the home of DJ Kool Herc, his real name is Clive Campbell. Campbell began the movement, and later hip-hop spread across the entire borough of the Bronx. Rap developed both inside and outside of hip-hop culture, and began in America starting with the street parties thrown in the Bronx neighborhoods of New York City. Campbell created the blueprint for hip-hop music and its culture by building upon the Jamaican tradition of boastful poetry and speech over music. This became emceeing, the rhythmic spoken delivery of rhymes and wordplay, delivered over a beat or without accompaniment. Campbell's syncopated, rhymed spoken accompaniment now known as rapping.

Jimmy's sparring sessions now, is always against the best fighter in Jimmy's weight class, Kenny Mitchell. When they both spar against each other they leave their heart and soul in the ring, and to see after their three rounds of pounding combinations of punches, blocking punches thrown at each other, it is beginning to look like art work. Jimmy learned to bob and weave at the right times after studying Kenny's boxing style to avoid being hit by Kenny's punches, and he also lands punches with his punching combinations that will land him extra points to a future tournament fight competition. Jimmy really learned the sport, and the feedback from Leon, and Chip were all instrumental. They became the larger part of Jimmy's support team. Jimmy now has the skill, speed, and strength in doing well in this upcoming Golden Gloves tournament. Leon and Chip both told me that Jimmy will do fine in this tournament, as long as he follows the boxing skills that he learned.

Chapter 10

First Match

Jimmy's personnel education in the sport of boxing at this point, with all his training has improved. Somehow, I had a premonition, after being with him and learning more about what makes him tick, and to witness his ability to deal with adversity, and how he shrugs off his every day demons, made me a believer. It takes a lot of courage to get into a boxing ring with another boxer who is trained in a New York sanctioned Golden Gloves gym. Jimmy always seemed sure of himself, I always try to observe his gestures, and listen to his feedback, and concerns to make sure that he understands what he is getting himself into. I also work on linking what's going on inside him to how he responds to his everyday training, to make sure he is all in. I noticed that his athleticism allows him to improve his boxing skills, confidence, and overall boxing

generalship. The humblest person could be a boxer. You get a guy off the streets that thinks he's a real badass and he comes in here, he's nobody. He's just another person, It's a skill. It's what you learn. It's the sacrifices, the training that will make him a Golden Gloves contender. Jimmy got notification for his first tournament fight, his first fight is located in the borough of Queens, New York. I contacted coach Chip from the Morrisania gym, and asked him if he has any other fighters from the Morrisania gym fighting their first fight at the Queens location where Jimmy is fighting? Chip knew right away who he was going to fight on this boxing card with Jimmy Gomez, because Morrisania Youth Center is an authorized sanctioned gym by the New York Golden Gloves and all sanctioned New York gyms are the first to be notified. Chip said, "yes I have fighters that will be fighting at that location that night. I'll be with you in Jimmy's corner"

These represented gyms are also notified as well as the attached and unattached boxers on the boxing card. All "unattached fighters" are not represented by a gym, they just train on their own at home. Very rarely do you hear of an unattached Golden Gloves fighter becoming a champion, if one ever did its rare. Jimmy's first match is against an unattached boxer. Sanctioned gyms offer excellent boxing training from retired boxers and it's all free training, and coaches that do it for the love of the sport to help guide the youths off the streets. Chip said, "Kenny Mitchell, and Davie Moore are fighting on the same card as Jimmy Gomez that evening. I will be there in the corner with you and Jimmy for his first fight." I told Chip, "ok, I appreciate it." I was relieved to have Chip around for Jimmy's first fight. The day before Jimmy's fight, I was going through all the necessary things Jimmy should do before tomorrow's fight. I told Jimmy, "rest the day before the fight, no training or running, just rest."

Jimmy sparred that entire week leading up to the pre-fight day. His body needed to recuperate, his weight is perfect, he is 1 pound under his maximum body weight for his weight class. I told him, "your body needs to recuperate from the hard work you did in preparation for this bout. So, rest." He tapered off that last week so his body can begin to recuperating. Also, "you're at a good weight, eat a small portion meal the night before. If you get hungry hydrate yourself drink lots of water to rid your urge to eat. You will need all of your energy during the fight not before and not after."

Thinking to myself, "I am so exhausted working my full-time job, then coaching Jimmy in the evening, with the long drive home from the South Bronx to Upstate New York." When I rested my head on my pillow that night it was lights out.

It came so fast, there we are, at the boxing arena in the evening. Jimmy checked in to weigh in, and to make sure he qualifies to fight in his designated light weight class. The Golden Gloves representative yelled out, “a possible disqualification Jimmy Gomez weighed in 2 pounds over his weight class!” Jimmy had 25 minutes to drop 2 pounds for a second and final chance to weigh in and qualify in his weight class or the fight becomes a loss/disqualification due to his overweight status. I told Jimmy to put on his sweat suit and jump rope before his next and final weigh in. While he is jumping rope, I became annoyed, and had to ask, “how did you gain 3 pounds in two days? I hope a lot of this weight is the water I told you to drink to stay hydrated.” Jimmy said, “I got hungry last night, and ate a hamburger and fries before I went to sleep,” he said, “I got hungry, I couldn’t help it, I did drink lots of water.” I said, “let’s hope that this excess weight is mostly water.” I could not believe Jimmy did this, after so much hard work, he put into keeping his weight down to compete in his weight class.

I was looking out for Chip and he has not arrived yet. I saw Leon just walking in with Davie Moore, and he said, "Chip had a late start leaving his fulltime job, but he will be here for Jimmy's first fight." I informed Leon that Jimmy indulged in a late-night burger and fries' cravings, now he has to work off 2 pounds to meet his official weight class. Leon said, "Jimmy's a tough kid, he will make his weight, at the same time he will learn his lesson on preparing for a Golden Glove's competition." I said, "I hope your right Leon, he needs to drop 2 pounds in time because he is scheduled to fight the first fight on the card." Chip gave me a lot of advice being Jimmy's handler, and so it looks like I may be alone with Jimmy's first fight because Chip may not arrive on time. While

Jimmy is sweating and jumping rope, he asked me if I've seen Chip yet, I said, "no, no problem, you and I got this fight. Chip left work a little later than usual and is on his way. Let's first take care of dropping those 2 lbs." Jimmy was jumping rope, and sweating, I was concerned that he will expend a lot of his energy that he needs for his fight. In the meantime, if he doesn't sweat off these 2 lbs. it's an automatic disqualifier, and he will lose the fight. I still see no sign of Chip, maybe he can share more about shedding this weight. He knows more about being in this situation, he warned me about this weigh-in part. I was hoping this didn't happen, but here we are trying to meet his weight class before his fight. I asked, "Jimmy can you urinate?" Jimmy said, "I'll try", he ran into the bathroom and release more body fluid, from what I heard from a distance, I was hoping it was the sound of him urinating, and not the sink water flowing. I yelled out to Jimmy, "here comes the tournament official!" The officials said to

Jimmy, "you have three-minutes remaining to get on the scale" I said, "ok Jimmy, keep jumping, keep sweating." Jimmy said, "I urinated a lot." The official is standing near the scale and he informs Jimmy to get on the scale. Jimmy takes off his sweats, he is drenched, I gave him a towel to wipe down the body sweat off his body before he got on the scale. He gets on the scale bare foot, wearing only his underwear. The tournament director yelled out, "you've met your weight to fight this tournament." Jimmy made a muscle pose after hearing the great news, smiles all the way around. I bandage and taped his hands; we had some time to rest. The rope jumping may have taken away some energy he needs for tonight's fight. I made sure he hydrated the water he lost to make weight, but it's good that he is sweating and already warmed up for his match.

Chip finally arrived and I updated him on Jimmy finally making his weight. Chip gave me a smile and a look as if to say, “I told you so.” Chip said, “these are the types of challenges a handler gets into with his fighters. You both took the right steps to rid his extra weight, good job.”

If Jimmy wins tonight’s fight, he will advance in the tournament, and will learn from this fight how to prepare better for his next fight.” The tournament representative calls out the first two boxers fighting tonight to begin walking to their perspective corners. This is the first time Jimmy gets to see his opponent. Jimmy and his opponent begin the march to the boxing ring and to their perspective corners of the ring at ringside. Jimmy’s opponent’s handlers were as young as his opponent, they looked like his neighborhood friends. Compared to the seasoned trainers from sanctioned gyms. When the announcer announced the boxer’s names. The ring announcer let the boxing fans know that Jimmy's opponent is unattached. The boxing fans knew that his opponent did not train in a sanctioned gym. This boxer trained on his own. Most of the unattached fighters are probably street fighters and enter the tournament thinking they are tough guys, a bad ass and somehow, they are going to put fear into their opponents to win. I reminded Jimmy that this guy is unattached, to keep your distance, and watch out for wild punches. Keep your hands up, when you see the opportunity stick him with straight hard jabs. When you see an opening begin throwing your combinations. I applied some Vaseline on Jimmy's face so any punches that landed on his face will more easily slide off the target, giving the punch less of an impact. The bell rings for the 1st round, Jimmy runs to the center of the ring to meet his opponent, and the opponent was not anxious to meet Jimmy head on. So, he got closer to his opponent and began throwing a couple of left jabs, and the opponent did not retaliate, still keeping his hands up, still no sign of any boxing skills from his opponent. Suddenly his opponent began throwing an enormous amount of wild punches. Jimmy was able to protect himself by sticking to his training techniques. His opponent gave away a lot about his boxing skills. His punches were thrown with no regard to protect himself. I yelled out “Jimmy counter punch, he’s open after he throws his punches” Jimmy began releasing his punches straight lefts and rights directly to his opponent’s face. Once His opponent was caught with a hard-right hand from Jimmy, his opponent began back peddling. Jimmy got caught with a couple of his opponent’s wild punches, but Jimmy shrugged those gazing blows off, and was able to bring his opponent to a defensive mode. Jimmy unleashing his groupings of very thought out combinations of punches that consisted of left hooks, uppercuts, left jabs and right cross. Towards the end of the 1st round, I could see Jimmy had total control of his opponent. Unattached fighters usually show their best in the 1st round, and his opponents round house punches implies that he doesn't have the skill set of a boxer. Sometimes unattached fighters get lucky and connect with wild punches, and if that happens, tonight could be lights out for Jimmy. Jimmy has not showed his abilities, because he is just being cautious, and is relying on his boxing skills to win this fight. You see, there is always a switch that Jimmy can turn on and that switch brings him back to a street fighter. We don't need that switch right now, because he is landing many blows and tallying up points in his favor. Sometimes In training when Jimmy gets frustrated, he gets so mad, because his boxing combinations are not working. He loses all boxing training techniques and begins throwing his barrage of very fast and accurate power punches. He brings each fist to the target on every punch, he focuses like a lion in the heat of battle. Jimmy has stopped many club fighters during his spar training. Knowing what I know, I say that Jimmy just finished a very good 1st round. Chip said to me, "let me say a few things to Jimmy, then you could have him the rest of the time." The bell rings to end the 1st round. Chip tells Jimmy, "that was a good 1st round, you only have two more rounds remaining to win this fight, this is not a professional fight where you can dance for 10 rounds, you get no points for dancing, this is the Golden Gloves you get points for connecting your punches. So, in this next round just keep punching, because every punch you land you get a point. The boxer with the most points wins this fight." While Chip gave Jimmy his feedback, I was giving Jimmy some water to spit out into the bucket. I spread more Vaseline on his face, washed out his mouth piece and put it in his mouth. I told Jimmy, "you backed him up and hurt him with your straight up the middle left right combinations. Make sure you bring your hands back to your face to guard it in case he throws one of his wild punches." Jimmy said, "I can't wait to get this guy out of here." The bell rings to begin the 2nd round. The opponent was slow to get up off his chair from his corner. Jimmy ran all the way over to his corner, and had the courtesy to wait until his opponent was ready by putting out his boxing glove to his opponent, they each tapped gloves, signifying their ready to begin the 2nd round. It's more of the same, Jimmy was delivering points by sticking his opponents lower and upper body punches, and his opponent was throwing his awkward over his head round house punches, the few that reached Jimmy were more like slaps. Suddenly Jimmy saw a short moment that his opponent dropped his guard to rest his arms, and Jimmy delivers two left hooks, one to his opponents right rib, then when his opponent lowered his right hand to protect his rib, Jimmy landed a left and a right cross to his jaw, then his opponents legs wobbled. The referee sees this immediately and tells Jimmy to go to his natural corner, he begins giving Jimmy's opponent a standing eight count. The opponent began yelling at the referee, "he didn't hurt me, I'm ok." The referee told his opponent, "you lost your balance after he punched you in your face." While Jimmy was waiting in the neutral corner for the eight count to end, I yelled out to Jimmy, "you hurt him, stay on him as soon as he finishes the eight count!" As soon as the referee finished his eight count to give his opponent time to recover, Jimmy runs over and starts throwing very hard punches. His punches were delivered with lots of speed, the opponent leaned against the ropes just protected his face, suddenly the bell rang to end the 2nd round. The bell saved the boxer. As soon as both boxers went to their respective corners to get their one-minute rest, I began tending to Jimmy. I let him know that he looks really good out there, but the fights not over. I told him, "you have to end this fight, while your opponent is still in a state of confusion, fear, and pain." When I looked over to his opponents' corner, there was a doctor with the referee, looking into the opponent's boxers' eyes with a small flashlight. I heard the opponent yelling, "don't stop the fight." I yelled to the referee, "Hey referee, stop this fight we don't want to send his opponent home more beat up than he currently is. He might wind up in the hospital." The fighter's handler said, "my fighter wants to fight another round." The referee asked the boxer, "do you want to continue to fight?" The opponent yelled out, "like I told you before, don't stop this fight, I'm ok, let me finish this fight!." The referee warned the fighter and the handler, "I'll let you continue to fight, but once I see that you are not fighting back, I will stop this fight." The handler and fighter agreed to his terms. I said to Jimmy, remember, throw the same combinations, left hooks to his ribs, then once your opponent drops his hand to protect his ribs, finish your combinations upstairs and go for the knockout, keep punching don't stop." The bell rings for the third and final round. Jimmy's opponent runs out to meet Jimmy in the center of the ring, and throws a couple of very weak left-hand jabs, Jimmy suddenly unleashes a barrage of powerful left hooks, right cross, one after another, he backs his opponent into the ropes after connecting with those punches. His opponent looked, scared and beaten and stopped throwing punches to retaliate. The referee, waved his hands, and yelled out, "I saw enough this fight is over." Jimmy wins the fight with a technical knockout. The fighter, was helped to his stool and the fight doctor was, tending to him. While Jimmy was jumping with his hands in the air. The referee asked Jimmy to come to the center of the ring, while the ring announcer announces, "By way of technical knockout, the winner from the Morrisania Youth Center, Bronx, NY, Jimmy Gomez." Jimmy began searching for me, looking around and suddenly made eye contact with me. Being extremely athletic he ran and leaped into my arms with a bear hug, to express his jubilant victory. After putting in all the hard work and dedication to the training, and the trust we have developed between us, his leaping bear hug said it all. Jimmy and I stayed to watch and support other Morrisania Gym boxers, and watched Davie Moore score a technical knockout victory, and Kenny Mitchell out pointed his opponent for a victory.

The next morning the New York Daily News, newspaper who are the sponsors of the New York Golden Gloves, filled the sports section with action photos of all of the fights, and reported the winners and losers. After Jimmy Gomez's stunning victory, he became very popular in his community, and with the New York Army National Guard. Street gang members began respecting Jimmy to have the heart to fight in the Golden Gloves, and all wanted to know him like they were always his friend. When I got into work, my phone was ringing off the hook. Everybody wanted me to know that last night's fight was covered in the New York Daily News, newspaper. Articles with Jimmy Gomez plus fight action photos were printed in the next morning sports section of the New York Daily News, newspaper.

Later that day I was called up to my supervisor's office, he was the Battalion Executive Officer. He immediately congratulated me for the extra off duty work Jimmy and I put into this project. I explained to my supervisor, "PFC Jimmy Gomez is a special soldier. He is stuck living in this poverty-stricken environment. He is trying to find a path to better his life, in doing so, he has been a good listener and we found an avenue for him. Boxing is building his confidence and hopefully will land him his GED, high school diploma, and a fulltime job. In the meantime, he is off the streets. By using his god given skill as a street fighter, he has been depending on me to help him find a way to connect his fighting skills to a brighter future. Hopefully this will land him a high school diploma which he is working on now. After he earns his GED, he has a better chance to get a job that earns him enough money to have his own apartment, living outside the South Bronx." The Executive Officer was all in, and wanted to let me know that his phone was ringing off the hook about our victory fight last night. The New York Army National Guard wanted to know more about Jimmy Gomez. I said, "great news sir, thank you."

I am not going to let this one victory get to Jimmy's head. We've got one more fight to win before he can enter the quarter finals, then one more fight to win to make it to the semi-finals, and if we win in the semi-finals, we will be fighting for the New York Golden Gloves champion ship match at Madison Square Garden on March 11, 1977. The New York Army National Guard wanted to be recognized for Jimmy Gomez's accomplishments. So, the soldiers and staff members of the 1st Battalion 105th Field Artillery all chipped in to buy Jimmy Gomez a custom boxing robe. The colors were red and gold the official colors of the First Battalion 105th Field Artillery. My first conversation with Jimmy the next day was mostly about reviewing his training plan for the week, and better ways to prepare for his next fight, light training, diet, and rest. Also, to make sure that he stays focused on his night classes for his GED. He told me he is all caught up with his studies, and finished his homework for his next class. I told Jimmy that your opponent was not as skilled as the sparring opponents you had at the gym. So, it looks like your next opponent who won his first fight is coming from a sanctioned gym out of Brooklyn, New York. Jimmy confident response was, “I’m hoping that my next fighter is more skilled, I’m looking for a challenge for my next fight.”

Chapter 11

Second Match

We have one week to get ready for Jimmy's second match which will be located in an armory in Queens, New York, a borough of New York City. Jimmy has now experienced his first Golden Glove Boxing match. When Chip is around, I give Chip the lead voice in our corner, Chip has taught me a lot about training a boxer, and I took my role as a corner man/coach very seriously to help Jimmy get an edge on winning. Chip showed me how to stop nose bleeds, and if needed to bandage a bleeding eye cut in a butter fly stich, Chip wanted to make sure I knew all of this in case he was unable to be in Jimmy's corner. The process of being ready for a Golden Gloves match can be difficult, but once we finished our first match, I understood the format of pre-fights, the actual fight, and post-fight responsibilities. Almost losing the first fight for showing up overweight was ridiculous. At times I felt that we were winging it, coming in overweight, coming very close to be eliminated from the competition. All that work that Jimmy put into getting prepared would have been thrown out the window. It was a good lesson for Jimmy. I put partial blame on myself as his trainer/coach. Was there something else I could have done to eliminate this additional stress on the boxer. To experience the actual crises of showing up to a fight overweight, is just about the best lesson you can imagine to make sure it won't happen again. So far at this point things just seem to be working out for Jimmy, almost like having a guardian angel watching over him.

I'm often asking him about the days away from the gym. I want him to be concentrating on his diet, and roadwork and at the same time attending evening courses to prepare him for a GED high school diploma. All these tasks that he is focused on, all equals the ultimate goal which is to keep him off the streets of the South Bronx, and on a positive path to an education and employment. I began almost sounding redundant by reminding him of our agreement.

Now it's time for preparation for his second match, it's good that Davie Moore and Kenny Mitchell from the same Morrisania gym are both on the same fight card. By winning their first match along with Jimmy this allowed them to advance in the tournament. Kenny who is Jimmy's favorite sparring mate weighs slightly more than Jimmy with a lot more ring experience, and puts him in a different weight class. This means they won't have to match Jimmy up against Kenny in this tournament. Kenny pretty much gives Jimmy sparring sessions that challenges him enough to be prepared to fight experienced fighters. Jimmy was actually disappointed in his first match by his opponents boxing skills. He wanted someone to give him a better challenge. I reminded Jimmy that the rest of the fighters remaining in the competition also won their first match and will be more skilled, and better than the unattached fighter he faced in his first fight.

When we got to the gym early in the week for training, we were met with Davie Moore's coach Leon Washington. Leon shared, "Hey Jimmy, I was observing your first match, even though your opponent was not as skilled as you, he could have been a dangerous opponent. If he made contact with one of his wild punches you could have been in trouble. I liked how you kept your guard up and stayed patient waiting for your opponent's openings. You delivered nice combinations with no wasted punches, a sign of a very good fighter." Jimmy never gave his opponent an opportunity to gain any positive momentum, and he delivered many accurate punches and collected many points, not many of Jimmy's punches were wasted, Leon was right. He appreciated Leon's positive words, coming from a retired professional fighter, and a boxing trainer at the Morrisania boxing gym. He thanked Leon for his encouraging words. He got into his workout routine, as he was warming up and jumping rope, a lot of boxers were giving acknowledgment to Jimmy's victory. I noticed that his mind set is more positive, coming off the win, his personality is much more robust, talking to amateur boxers around the gym during their one-minute rest session. Jimmy was feeling like being more open about himself, and establishing new friends.

His next match is five days away, I'm still thinking about the existing fighters that are remaining in the tournament in Jimmy's weight class. I was figuring they along with Jimmy feel they will be the next Golden Gloves champ. I reminded Jimmy that we are on track with his training program for his next fight, and let's take each training day and every day from here on out, one day at a time. Jimmy's endurance and strength improved as he increased the frequency of his sparring sessions and his miles to his morning road work to six miles a day. This week or at least for the next four days before his fight Jimmy worked harder than he had ever worked to prepare for his 2nd fight. Each day he sparred with Kenny, and a couple of other gym boxers.

We found out through Chip who knows many of the boxing trainers in the local New York City boxing gyms that Jimmy's next match is a boxer that scored a knockout in his first fight last week. He is an attached boxer from the Castle Hill AC gym in the East Bronx, New York. Many very good amateurs and professional fighters train in this gym, and we are expecting Jimmy's opponent to be prepared for this match. Chip told me that all the fighters coming out of the Castle Hill AC gym have a history of being tougher, smarter, and skilled opponents. These boxers are a lot more disciplined than the average amateur boxer. Jimmy is a much different fighter than he was when he first started training, and I also believe that he is also much smarter, stronger and extremely disciplined, if you count out his debacle of coming in overweight, which almost cost him an elimination loss. Based merely on how he handled himself on his first fight, Jimmy should give his next opponent a run for his money, and beat him. I always stayed optimistic; Jimmy's demeanor in the ring is one that shows, he believes in himself, and I believe in him.

There was no pre-fight hiccups, Jimmy made weight, his hands taped up, and gloves fit snug, and warmed up to fight. The bell rings to begin the 1st round. Jimmy's opponent is extremely athletic and he was quick on his foot work. His left jab that landed frequently kept Jimmy away from landing punches. His opponent used his long arm reach to score points with straight hard jabs. Jimmy showed signs of frustration, his rhythm the entire 1st round was thrown off, because his opponent did a very good job of sticking his left hand to Jimmy's face. The entire 1st round his opponent out punched him. Jimmy clearly lost the 1st round. His opponent dominated with speed and crisp punches. The bell rings to end the 1st round. Jimmy showed up in his corner with a bleeding nose, and a knot forming above his right eye, a possible head butt, not sure. While I was working on stopping the blood flow from all those left jabs he received, Jimmy asked, if he won the 1st round. I said, "no you didn't, you're too anxious, you are signaling your right-hand punch to your opponent. This guy is a boxer, calm down and find an opening to get closer and land combinations and quickly back off. Use your legs, move more to your left, and keep your hands up to protect your face. Once you find your opening, don't stop punching. Jimmy seemed overwhelmed over the opponents boxing skills. Chip said, "son that's not you fighting out there, are you afraid of him?" Jimmy said, "Hell No" "then give me the work and muscle you show at the gym, get inside and don't stop punching." When the bell rang for round 2, Jimmy got back into a defensive mode waiting for an opening to deliver his combo. His opponent's footwork and speed of his jabs, was too much for Jimmy to counter punch. All of a sudden, his opponent showed signs of exhaustion, he couldn't keep the fast pace he has been using. Is this a bad day for Jimmy, because at this point he is falling behind on his way to losing this fight. Suddenly, halfway through the round, Jimmy noticed his opponent's legs and arms were tiring, and his opponent decided to do a “peak a boo” style defensive, buy putting his gloves in front of his face and resting his back against the ropes. His opponent probably felt that he is winning the fight and wanted to coast his way to the end by resting. Jimmy began to land very powerful right left crosses on his face, then left jabs and hooks to his ribs followed by his right cross. Jimmy sees his opportunity, and let go of his arsenal of combinations, his opponent continued to block some of them, but some landed for points and pain. I yelled, “That’s the Jimmy I know, Keep punching!” You can see that his opponent was tired and wincing after Jimmy lands his punches. The referee gave his opponent a time out and a warning, “If you continue not to return punches to show me that you’re still willing to fight, I will stop this fight.” The bell rings to end the 2nd round. Chip told me, “I’m not sure how the Judges will score that round some of Jimmy’s punches at the end of this round were blocked by either the opponents boxing gloves, or his arms. I'm sure though that Jimmy is losing this fight with only one round to go." Chip was serious thinking Jimmy might lose this fight. I told Chip, "let me talk to him this round." While Chip tended to washing out Jimmy's mouth piece and greasing his face to get ready for the 3rd and final round. I stood in front of Jimmy and said, "look at me, and pay attention, I raised the volume of my voice to a level that I knew he was paying attention. I said, "with all the hard work you put into this fight, and all the soldiers that are watching you and supporting you, you need to do something different to beat this guy!" Now I'm yelling at him and said, "you got this guy hurt, and you are losing this fight, he is blocking a lot of your punches. You have to get inside his jabs and knock his ass out!" He looked at me with eyes wide open, in a way that his life was on the line. It was a desperate stare that he understood, and that he needed to do something desperately. The best description I could describe is when the bell rang for the 3rd and final round. Jimmy the boxer didn't answer that bell, that's right! It was Jimmy the street fighter that answered the bell. When that bell rang Jimmy jumped off his corner stool, ran over to his opponents' corner and was waiting for his opponent to get off his stool. The referee noticed that Jimmy's opponent and handlers were slow answering the bell. They were still giving last minute instructions after the bell rang for the last round. The referee called time out and gave the opponents corner a warning, "I will disqualify your fighter for not answering the bell on time, come on let's go!" The referee grabbed both fighters by their gloves and walked them to the center ring, as soon as the referee let go of both Jimmy and his opponents' gloves and gave the verbal and hand signal, "fight." Jimmy immediately landed a left hook to his opponent's jaw while his opponent was on his way down to the canvas jimmy landed a right cross that was already in flight being followed up after his left cross. It's hard to stop a left, right combination when the left has already landed. Both punches landed, the referee immediately waved both hands to signify the fight is over for boxer's safety rather than counting him out. Jimmy was jumping up and down in celebration, meanwhile Chip a seasoned gym boxing coach stayed humble, and said to me, "you have a special fighter in Jimmy." the whole crowd in this venue was all on their feet yelling cheering, and clapping, knock downs are exiting to boxing fans.

Then came the official announcement, the ring announcer announces win by technical knockout and raises Jimmy's arm. Then he began scanning the ring looking for me. He does his traditional leap and bear hug into my arms in the center of the ring, a celebration for his second victory. Jimmy's conditioning has made the difference. The miles of roadwork, the hours of sparring, the discipline of the military, and the many years of his survival street fighting has contributed to this insurmountable victory.

Chapter 12

Quarter Finals

Drawing from New York City's five boroughs, New York City has always had a deep pool of boxing talent. The amateur boxing system in New York has always found a way to tap into those reservoirs of talent. During the 1970's neighborhood boxing gyms flourished in lower Manhattan, Harlem, the Bronx and various Brooklyn neighborhoods. The young men who wanted to test themselves in the ring could always find a place close to home. This has dwindled down with the decrease of small neighborhood gyms. There were around 150 neighborhood gyms within the five boroughs of New York City, and today there is less than 50. It's a shame for this decrease because today more than ever we need back that avenue for street youths to save themselves. School counselors, police officers, mothers with troubled son's,

the penal system, have used the local boxing gym as a choice to try to save a troubled youth. It is still the sport of the lower social economic level of New York because it helps kids become disciplined and productive. It's a way to get their aggression level down in a positive way. After speaking with a few New York City beat cops, I learned that it was common for a beat cop to grab misbehaving kids and toss them into a boxing ring of their own called the Police Athletic League – PAL, rather than a jail cell in an effort to giving them one more chance. It's all about discipline, physical fitness, camaraderie, and team. It teaches street youths work ethics.

When it comes to the sport of boxing from a coaching view point, I'm counting on Jimmy's street experience as a fighter as it relates to his perseverance to experience victory. A place where the street culture believed a man who couldn't use his fists couldn't call himself a man. Even the councilors, priests and some teachers knew how to throw a punch. Jimmy was born with heavy fists, and a solid chin. Lots of youths his age while growing up might hesitate to punch with all their might, he used all his strength. Other youths might flinch when presented with the opportunity to strike someone in the face. Gomez aimed his fists directly at his opponents' nose, where a punch would hurt the most and result with spurting blood. At times Jimmy was the receiver in some exchanges and could take a punch. Speed and athleticism are import attributes, but Jimmy excels in gameness the very part of one of his stronger attributes of bravery and courage.

After winning two matches in this tournament, Jimmy is now qualified for entry into the 1977 New York Daily News Quarterfinals. He knows he has his work cut out for him especially after facing a very good boxer in his last match. His last opponent owned a boxing style that could have beat Jimmy. His conditioning, tenacity, courage, and perseverance allowed him to prevail with a come from behind knockdown, that led to a very impressive victory.

This is Jimmy's first year in the Golden Gloves, fighters in their first year in this tournament fall into their own league called the novice, his favorite sparring partner Kenny Mitchell out of the Morrisania Youth center is also in his first year in the New York Daily News Golden Gloves Tournament. He is also registered as a novice fighter along with Jimmy. Davie Moore also out of the same Morrisania gym was a 1st time 1976 novice Golden Gloves Champion. This tournament Davie is registered into the open category as he is competing against boxers in the open class. The open league are all those boxers that have already competed in this tournament in previous years.

After every Golden Gloves tournament match the New York Daily News publishes results and action photos of the fighters in the sports section of the newspaper. At this point he has an enormous following, his friends and his prior foes from street gangs. Everyone wanted to be Jimmy's friend. The New York Army National Guard wanted interviews to print in their next month's military magazine. Everyone knew who Jimmy Gomez was, and Jimmy loves every moment of his success. I began getting contacts from young soldiers, asking me to train them for next year's Golden Gloves. I invited all those prospective military amateur boxers to join a local boxing gym in their neighborhoods. I informed them that there is no cost to participate. There are plenty of experienced volunteer coaches that are willing to help youths become amateur boxers. It's not as easy as they think it is, fighters need to have motivation, heart, and a sheer desire to step into that ring to battle another opponent.

One evening after finishing a sparring session, Jimmy said, "once this tournament is over and I win my Golden Gloves championship award, I will wear my golden gloves award every day for the rest of my life. I will never step in a ring again to fight, because I don't like fighting." Those were powerful words that Jimmy expressed. Words that revealed his confidence in his fighting ability to be the next champ, coupled with his sense of wellbeing in knowing when to stop. He has a vision of being off the streets, educated and employed and this future has no place for fighting. It was plain to see by now that Jimmy has the "tiger instinct" that is a necessary attribute for a boxing champion, but he also has the intelligence, freedom and realization to select a life of his own.

Here we are at ring side Jimmy disrobed his gifted military red and gold Army Artillery colored robe and wearing his red and gold boxing trunks. Tonight's opponent is a trained attached fighter out of a Harlem, New York City gym. After the introductions the bell rings to begin the 1st round. Jimmy is becoming more of a seasoned boxer; he first feels out his opponent. Jimmy jumped in and threw a straight jab, and jumped out quickly to see his opponent's reaction. His opponent has not thrown a punch, the crowd was beginning to make booing sounds because they want to see punches thrown, not foot work. New York sport fans come to a venue to see action. So, Jimmy repeated the same foot work, but this time when he jumped in, he delivered a left and right that were direct hits to his opponent's jaw. His opponent tried to counter Jimmy's punches but was awkward and off balance then grabbed Jimmy's arms trying to somehow rest because he may have gotten dazed by Jimmy's punches. Jimmy was looking very good, and now is showing signs of controlling the fight in the 1st round. With about 25 seconds remaining in the 1st round, Jimmy began a vicious assault startling his opponent with a left hook to his stomach, and then he followed it up with a left to his opponent's head. As his opponent's right hand protected his head, Jimmy's right hand was levitating down by his waist waiting for an opening to strike with the right hand. Jimmy fired the right hand with sudden swiftness, landing it flush against his opponent's jaw. The referee saw his opponent was shaken by Jimmy's right hand; he gave him a standing eight count to give him time to recover. After the eight count the referee asked the boxer, "are you ok?" his opponent replied and said, "yes." He asked the boxer to walk towards him, and the boxer did without any swaying in his steps. His opponent was temporarily stunned by the power and precision of Jimmy's right hand. The referee gave the signal to box, this also is letting the time keeper know to let the time clock continue to run. Jimmy was on him quickly and began to chase his opponent around the ring like a leopard chasing an elephant. His opponent was stumbling from one corner to the other, clutching at the ropes. He was warned by the referee to take his hands off the ropes. The bell rang to end the 1st round, his opponent was saved by the bell. When Jimmy returned to his corner, he was feeling good about the 1st round. I told Jimmy, “take deep breathes, your opponent is hurt stay on top of him. Be careful, keep your distance, watch for his counterpunch, keep your gloves high to protect yourself.” The bell rings to start the 2nd round. Jimmy ran to the center of the ring and his opponent did the same, they were both exchanging punches, Jimmy’s punches were landing much more accurately. Several times they were entangled and once they both fell to the ground. Jimmy was the first to get back up to his feet. Jimmy eased back for the remaining 2nd round, he was surprised that he could not produce a knockout after striking many rights and lefts to his opponent's face. The bell rings to end the 2nd round. His opponent was much taller than he is, in fact all of Jimmy's fighters have been taller than him. He is pretty much always the shorter fighter even in the gym against his sparring partners, but he packs a power punch that is stronger than those fighters in his weight class. Whenever his opponents at the gym, and in the tournament were fighting each other in the ring, the disparity in the height between them disappeared. Jimmy's punching power equalized the disparity. Jimmy fought standing erect, while his opponent had to slouched to reach him. This made it easier for Jimmy to hit their chin with an upper cut. Chip and I felt that Jimmy may have lost the 2nd round because his opponent revived from his 1st round. Jimmy laid back too long in this round waiting for an opening, even though Jimmy was blocking a lot of his opponent's punches, some were able to reach Jimmy not enough power to hurt him, but definitely enough power to score points. The bell rings to end the 2nd round. Jimmy looks refreshed and confident, but we let him know that your opponent may have out pointed you that 2nd round. The bell rings to start the 3rd and final round. Jimmy landed a right hand that toppled his opponent, but he got up quickly, and received a standing eight count. about 1 minute and 30 seconds into the 3rd round Jimmy landed 2 left hooks to his opponents' stomach which brought down his arms to protect his ribs, and suddenly Jimmy sees an opening and lands a crushing right hand to his opponent's jaw. That crushing right hand knocked down his opponent again, and he tried to get up, but his legs were rubbery. Chip yelled out to the referee, "stop the fight ref!" The referee saw what Chip saw an exhausted and hurt boxer. The referee stopped the fight, making Gomez a winner by a technical knockout. Seconds later Jimmy ran over to his opponent to make sure he was ok, and they both hugged each other as a sign of good sportsmanship. Then the ring announcer takes Jimmy's hand and lifts his arm to signify the winner of the quarterfinal lightweight match. The announcement, "winner in the quarterfinals in the lightweight division, from the Morrisania Youth Center, Jimmy Gomez!" Jimmy scanning the ring and when he saw me, ran and leaped into my arms for our traditional victory bear hug celebration. His opponent never gave up, he always got to his feet never wanting to quit. He never asked the referee to stop the fight. His opponents face became red and swollen from Jimmy's punches. I was glad for fighter safety that the fight was stopped. Another great win for Jimmy, his amateur record is now 3 wins and 0 losses. Jimmy now qualifies for the New York Daily News Golden Gloves Semifinals.

Chapter 13

Semifinals

Jimmy now is training on auto pilot since he recently increased his training running miles, and the amount of sparring boxing rounds, he has been training more than he has in the past, because of his increased endurance, and motivation. He became physically fit and in very good condition to fight and win in this tournament. His continued physical and mental boxing training within the Morrisania gym, running long miles through the streets of the war-torn South Bronx, seemed to make him stronger with each workout. After his intense training, he occasionally mentions his muscle aches due to his intense training activities. Suddenly when he hit the heavy bag, he expected to wince. When the pain stopped coming, he almost missed it. His body became use to all the training he puts into his body. It had been with him for so long while his muscles were growing. Slowly though, he grew accustomed to punching without pain. Eventually when the pain receded in his thoughts, he began to punch harder than he had. He had never really noticed how the muscle growing pain had inhibited his punching power. I also noticed, in his sparring sessions, he does not waste punches, he saves his left jabs the ones he used to paw with, they are now strategic quick hard landing jabs that are mostly used when there is an opening and he will reach his target with it. His right hand became his big gun, more like heavy Artillery shells landing on his target. His footwork became faster to help him avoid being hit while he was bobbing and weaving to avoid his opponents' punches. The running of great distances has increased his stamina in this short period of time of a couple of months. In his previous fights when he got hit with punches, they are hardly the hard punches. He doesn't take the others on purpose, but it just seems that when the hard ones come whistling at him, he ducks, blocks, and quickly moves away. His sense of reading his opponents big punches has improved with the rest of his ring generalship. With four days to go for his next semifinal fight in the New York Daily News Golden Gloves tournament, he wished the fight was tomorrow instead of Friday. He wanted to climb in the ring while he still felt this good. He wouldn't have to spend another four days waiting for possibly one of the biggest events of his life. The next morning the New York Daily News was beginning to fill stories about the upcoming semifinal fights. In days leading up to this next fight I kept on receiving phone calls, and visits from military personnel, and especially higher headquarters. Most of the phone calls and visits were to express hope that Jimmy Gomez will be a Golden Gloves Champion. Through these final days before the semifinal fight Gomez seems to be the

only calm and collected person compared to his stable mates training entourage. Jimmy hides his anxiety, but I seem to wear mine on my sleeve. Jimmy Gomez, Davie Moore, and Kenny Mitchell, and a light heavy weight fighter by the name of Johnny Hayes are all undefeated fighters from the Morrisania gym. During a training evening at the gym a small crowd of boxing fans, sports writers, and photographers were there to greet these boxers, the boxers were treated like celebrities. Jimmy Gomez was being recognized as being in tip top physical condition. When he sparred with Kenny Mitchell, he seems to have gotten much quicker and graceful than ever before. Maybe the small crowd that flooded the gym may have put Jimmy into his game day mental state. He did have his game face on, and he looked great.
Comments from coaches that night all agreed that Jimmy transformed into an entirely newer fighter, with much

more definition to his physical appearance and ring generalship. Meaning that he is now dictating his own pace, style, space and tactics of a bout.

Jimmy is up against an undefeated fighter like himself who trained at the lower east side, AC gym in New York City. This fighter is undefeated as all semi-finalists are, a much taller opponent as all his opponents have been with a longer arm reach, as the elimination tournament pack is dwindling down, his competition gets more challenging.

Its fight night, I told Jimmy that once again you're going to be dealing with a fighter with a longer arm reach, so be ready to jump inside his punches like you did in your previous fight. Jimmy said, "I got this." He is warmed up and his gloves are laced up, we were told that in 15 minutes be ready to enter the ring. All pre-fight requirements are done. I was keeping Jimmy positive, and staying optimistic just as we were from the very first fight. If Jimmy beats this opponent, he will be on to the big stage in Madison Square Garden for the 1977 Golden Gloves Championship match. I put out my two fists and Jimmy like a sludge hammer hit my fists with his gloves, he is zoning into the moment. He has his game face on and his stare that makes me feel that he is at his ready state to fight. Jumping up and down in a rhythmic movement, to keep warm, beads of sweat is on his forehead, always a good sign. Wearing his Army gold and red robe, Artillery colors, that was gifted to him by the soldiers of the 1st Battalion 105th Artillery. We got the signal to enter into the ring, and as we walked a path to reach the ring, I was amazed of the large crowd that filled this boxing event, a crowd of boxing fans that acknowledged Jimmy as if they knew more about his journey. Being a military man, and reaching this level in the semi-finals, New York City boxing fans began clinging to the patriotic side and for Jimmy and hoping he wins the entire tournament. Jimmy gave a couple of acknowledgments by raising a glove in the air, but he is zoned in and ready to battle. After they announced both fighters and the referee go over the rules in the ring for presentation. They also go over the official rules with the boxers in the locker room before every fight. The rules that are given to the boxers in the ring is only part of the boxing entertainment package for the boxing fans watching the fight. The referee said, "tap gloves and good luck at the bell come out fighting." Jimmy gets some more guidance from Chip and I before the bell rings to start the 1st round. The bell rings to start the 1st round. The opponent meets Jimmy in the middle of the ring and begins throwing left jabs followed by a right cross, these punches surprised Jimmy as he back pedaled and lower his head, not punching just trying to block his punches. This was going on for almost the first half of the 1st round.

Then Jimmy being the shorter fighter, he ducked one time and faced down toward the ring mat, his opponent landed punches on top and in the back of Jimmy's head. The referee called time out to stop the clock, and warned his opponent, "don't hit the back of the head it's an illegal blow, that is your final warning, I will tell the judges to add penalty points to your score card if you do it again." The stop gave Jimmy time to reevaluate, he looked over at our corner for guidance, and both Chip and I yelled, "start punching back, punch, punch, combinations" his opponent realized that by throwing these non-stop wild punches, Jimmy had no time to punch back, and he only used his gloves to deflect the barrage of punches thrown. I noticed his opponents' handlers during the stop yelling at their fighter, "get back in their keep up the pressure." It seems that they were trying for a 1st round knockout. When the referee gave the hand signal to fight, his opponent ran right after jimmy, and began throwing his wild punches, Jimmy refrained himself from turning this into a street brawl and his next move shows the boxing patients and skills he learned in the gym. His opponent fired a right cross towards Jimmy's left temple, and suddenly with Jimmy's quickness and strength ducked his head while studying his opponents movements, the right cross went sailing in the wind above his head, then Jimmy with his left arm strength pushed his opponents right side and with the momentum of his opponents right cross combined with Jimmy's left arm strength, he was able to turn his opponent around, while his opponent was off balance and still turning in a 360 degree, Jimmy had a right cross in flight waiting for him for impact. This punch drove his opponent back against the neutral corner of the ring. While his opponent was back pedaling and trying to find his steady balance his senses were clear enough to realize that he needed to hold both gloves by his face to block punches. Jimmy wasted no punches, he stood low, and delivered about 6 to 7 left and right hooks to his opponents' ribs, and abs. Once his opponent brought his elbows low enough to protect his ribs, he immediately went upstairs to strike his opponents face. Jimmy threw a right-hand upper cut that landed perfectly to his opponent's chin, and I thought that punch would end the fight. It didn't, Jimmy was throwing very affective blows and combinations to the stomach, then upstairs to the head. It was coming close to the end of the 1st round, and Jimmy did not let him out of the corner, his continued left hooks and right crosses made him regain points value to take back the 1st round. The bell rings to end the 1st round. When Jimmy returned to his corner and sat on the stool, he said that his opponent throws hard punches, my response was, "you throw harder punches, and that was a great move turning him around and throwing those combinations. Your opponent is tired, and now respects your punching power." Chip said, "keep getting to the inside, and throw combinations downstairs to his stomach and ribs, then ending upstairs to his head, just like you were doing." Jimmy gave me a head nod, I Vaseline his face, and put his mouth piece in his mouth, the bell rings to start the 2nd round. Jimmy's opponent had no answers for the second half of the 1st round. Suddenly his opponent seemed rejuvenated in the start of the 2nd round, by landing two quick left jabs to Jimmy's head. Jimmy stepped back to regroup and did not show any noticeable effect by his opponent's punches. As the fight advanced frustration was setting in on Jimmy, I could see it. He was respecting his punching power. As his opponents lead begins to pile, Jimmy seemed to resolve to fight carefully, so he won't get knocked out. His opponent also decided to develop a slower fighting pace, and seemed to want to rest himself. Suddenly Jimmy strikes his opponent with a very hard right cross to the temple. His opponents' knees buckled and he staggered ever so slightly. For a moment it seemed that his opponent was going to topple over. The crowd all rose as one to see the effect Jimmy's punch had on his opponent. Suddenly his opponent was back in his fighting stance, he threw a punch at Jimmy's head, missing high, then his opponent moved in and landed several body blows. Jimmy responded with terrific speed and power with counter combinations, 2 left hooks to the ribs, followed by a left cross and a right cross to his opponent's face. His opponent looked shell shocked and Jimmy went in to finish him off. While his opponent was back pedaling on his heals, and holding his gloves up by his face to protect his face, Jimmy began throwing combinations to his stomach and face like a machine gun, just nonstop punching, The bell rings to end the 2nd round, the referee jumps in between the fighters to end the fighting of the 2nd round. When Jimmy sat on his stool to rest in between rounds, Chip told Jimmy, "Son, this is an amateur fight there is no time to rest and dance around, you only have 1 round to prove to the judges that you are the better fighter, so get in there and keep punching . I told Jimmy, "Chip is right, there is no telling how the judges are going to score this fight, so get in there and knock this guy out. Jimmy gave me the nod."

The bell rings to start the 3rd and final round Jimmy struck first by landing a long-left jab to his opponent's face. His opponent hit Jimmy with a solid body shot, but Jimmy responded immediately with three very quick and hard right hands to his opponent's head, Jimmy showed no sign of being hurt after getting hit with his opponent's solid body shot. His opponent continued with his flurry of punches, and Jimmy joined the battle with his flurry of punches. The fight now is in full speed, both fighters are punching going for a knockout. Both fighters came this far, and it's the final round, they both know what is at stake. His opponent lands a left hook directly to Jimmy's chin. This punch made Jimmy realize that this fighter is a tough guy, and he could deliver and take a power punch. Jimmy looked over for a split second at our corner, and both Chip and I are yelling at Jimmy to throw punches, combinations, box. There is about 30 seconds remaining in this round, and Jimmy needs to keep punching to land points to win this fight. Jimmy steps back for a breather, dances for about 5 seconds, and decides to turn on the heat, his street fighter switch. Jimmy jumps back into the mix of this brawl and delivers two picture perfect upper cuts to his opponent's chin. The first upper cut jolted his opponents head back, and his opponent drops his gloves to his waist sides the crowd stood up waiting for a knockout, but his opponent recovered and began counter punching by throwing wild punches, and missing his targets a sign that he is desperate because he is hurt. Jimmy finds his openings to deliver and land his combinations until the bell rings to end the fight. Chip and I both agreed before the results were announced, that Jimmy's ending of the fight landed him a victory, but the fight game sometimes is seen differently through the eyes of judges. You just never know what the judges saw.

The judges turn in their score cards, and the ring announcer reads the judges results, "it was a unanimous decision for the winner out of the Morrisania Gym in the Bronx, Jimmy Gomez." Jimmy advances to the New York Daily News Golden Gloves Championship match at Madison Square Garden. The referee raises Jimmy's hand. This time I was out of the ring jumping with pride over Jimmy's victory with the ring side crowd, Jimmy's ceremonial athletic leap and bear hug celebration has a possibility to be postponed because the crowds were

blocking me to enter the ring. As soon as I get to finally jump through the ropes to join Jimmy in the ring, I turn around with my back to the ropes. There he was already in flight for our bear hug celebration. He landed with my back against the ropes, he yelled out, "we did it! we did it!." I told him, "you're the fighter, you did it! You're going to the Finals! congratulations."

Trust

On my way home in my car driving from the semifinal victory match, I began thinking about what makes our relationship boxer-coach work so well? Is it the military pride and respect that comrades in arms have for each other? Well I'm sure that was a factor. What is this formula that we are using that is working so well with each other and resulting in so much success? If I knew what it was, I would bottle it, and become a successful entrepreneur. It's too easy for me to use the word faith, I am a believer of faith, a strong belief in God and doctrine of religion. Sometimes I 've heard people use the word faith as trusting someone, in example: "I have faith in someone" Faith and trust are contradictory. Faith has been related to the substance of hope. But trust is real, it's something you can see, feel and touch. Trusting someone means that you think they are reliable; they continuously show it to you day in and out. You have confidence in them and you feel safe with them physically and emotionally. When Jimmy was involved in a street fight and Police Officer Smith asked Jimmy, "can I call a family member to verify your alibi?" Jimmy told Police Officer Smith, "I only trust Mr. Ron Sardanopoli to verify my alibi" it was then that I knew that Jimmy had trusted me," It also helped me to begin building my trust in him. Trust is something that Jimmy and I have been building together while working together in the military and one on one on his boxing journey.

If I had to coach a boxer that I didn't trust and the boxer didn't trust me, it would be challenging and draining. It's like putting together a group of people, working together often making disappointing progress, they may not share important information, they may battle over mistakes and whose fault it is. The bottom line is, if there is no cooperation with each other in a non-trusting environment, in our case the boxing team members may not reach its full potential.

Jimmy began learning how to step away from the inner-city streets, a hornet's nest filled with non-trusting people. They are looking in the wrong places for a future for themselves. Jimmy began working with strong military leaders and mentors when he joined the Army National Guard. When he joined the Army National Guard, he was introduced to the idea of trusting his comrades in arms. When soldiers team up for a mission, they all do it for one reason and one reason only, and that's for the love and freedom of their homeland. It was a faraway idea compared to the education one gets growing up in the streets of the South Bronx. I observed Jimmy as well as other young soldiers, and how they interacted with military team members. Jimmy cautiously picked small conversation with some soldiers, but he mostly kept busy almost to try to avoid any negative interaction with anyone. He surrounded himself with team leaders and basically those specific people that he needed to trust to accomplish the team's military missions. I believe that is where he got introduced to trusting people and learned to develop his part into being a successful team player.

When you sign an agreement as a citizen soldier with the Army National Guard for six years, and you attend all of your obligated duty which is one weekend a month and two weeks in the summer months, you satisfy your obligation. The problem that Jimmy has is, the balance of those non duty days, weeks, and months puts Jimmy backout on the streets of the South Bronx. He becomes a civilian that is unemployed, and a high school dropout.

The only time Jimmy surrounded himself in a more trusting environment is when he attended his mandatory Army National Guard duty days.

Jimmy's decision to choose the boxing ring as a new road to make change in his life was a perfect decision for him. He is now boxing, working on his high school diploma – GED, and pursuing employment all at the same time. The greatest part about this whole formula is he is no longer hanging out on the streets of the South Bronx. He positioned himself for a future to become economically successful.

Jimmy is Puerto Rican American and I am Italian American. Another social cultural challenge with our boxer-coach relationship. We came from different international cultures. A multicultural collaboration requires a plan, lots of patience, and determination to confront old attitudes in new ways. Our multicultural collaboration became affective, the people involved with us overcame their differences to promote a unified effort. Because of our different skill levels, expertise, and cultures our collaboration seemed uneven at first. For example, when I was invited to take on responsibilities of being a boxer's coach at the Morrisania gym, I felt that was out of my area of knowledge. Others may want to scapegoat that position in case things don't work. I decided to take that responsibility with open arms, I kept my focus on the common goal. Jimmy and I stayed close and worked hand in hand with the experienced, trusting coaches and trainers at the gym. We shared decision making, defined our roles, and set time lines. Jimmy and I together with our multicultural support team consisting of Puerto Rican/American, Italian/American and African American (gym coaches), were all in on our plan. We were also part of their plan to make it work for all of us. Now,

Jimmy is surrounded by a larger team of trusted coaches and trainers that hold a powerful formula to make him a Golden Gloves Champion.

Chapter 15

The Big Stage

The ultimate goal of every professional boxer is to win a world title, but running a close second is the opportunity to be featured in a main event at the world's most famous sports arena—Madison Square Garden. On the evening of March 11, 1977 Jimmy Gomez gets the opportunity to feature himself on the big stage in Madison Square Garden, New York City. He is being offered a chance to earn the title of the New York Daily News 1977 Golden Gloves Championship. Jimmy has given his boxing fans explosive entertaining fights in his previous fights. The New York Daily News now refer to him as, Jimmy "Big Gun" Gomez as he wears his robe and gear showing his red and gold Artillery colors representing his military organization, 1Bn. 105th Field

Artillery. Numerous future professional world champions have participated in the 92-year-old Daily News Golden Gloves, including international Boxing Hall of Famers Emile Griffith, Jose Torres, and Floyd Paterson.

New York City being the largest city in the state of New York and the United States, has the most sports fans per capita. This puts Jimmy's fight in a spot light media large enough to attract sports media newspapers, TV, including ESPN.

Jimmy Gomez's opponent for the championship bout on Friday, March 11, 1977 is Fernando Linares. Fernando is fighting out of the sanctioned Yonkers PAL, also undefeated. Jimmy is facing a boxer that is taller than him with a much longer arm reach. Jimmy's most dominant attribute is his, power, and muscular frame, which gives him the punching power that he uses when he reaches down deep, or when his life depends on it. I've watched Fernando Linares box during Jimmy's previous matches. Fernando is a very good boxer; his overall ring generalship is very good. He is a gamer just like Jimmy, I've watched his boxing athleticism, he is a balanced fighter with very fast foot work, his long reaching arms combined with his combination punching power makes him a very difficult opponent. Fernando has a solid chin; he does not get alarmed when he gets hit with a strong punch because of his strong chin. Fernando belongs in the finals along with Jimmy, and I have a feeling that he will give Jimmy the fight of his life.

On the night of our road trip from the Morrisania Youth Center Gym, Bronx, N.Y. to Madison Square Garden, New York City, for the 1977 New York Daily News Golden Gloves tournament. There was a total of four boxers who were still in the tournament for the championship match from the sanctioned Morrisania Youth Center gym. Jimmy Gomez, Davie Moore, and Kenny Mitchell, and a light heavy weight by the name of Johnny Hayes. All four boxers were on the same card that night. We all agreed to meet at the Morrisania gym to head out to Madison Square Garden together. When we all met at the gym Davie Moore's coach Leon Washington asked me if I could give him and Davie Moore a lift to the Garden. Leon was having car problems and couldn't get it started. I said, "oh most definitely yes." Leon sat in the passenger seat, and Jimmy and Davie were in the back seats. Chip who was Kenny Mitchell's coach transported Kenny and Johnny in his car and followed us downtown into the borough of Manhattan where Madison Square Garden is located. During the car ride, Leon was praising Jimmy and Davie for reaching this far into the competition, "no matter what happens tonight Jimmy and Davie, you should hold your heads high after the match." Davie said, I'll be holding my head high because I will be the next two-time champ," and Jimmy chimed in, and said, "I can't wait to knockout my opponent." Leon and I both smiled and I said, "now that's what we wanted to hear." On our ride to the Garden, Leon was sharing his own personal history of his boxing career, "Davie Moore reminded me of myself when I was an amateur boxer." Leon felt that he had very bad managers as he entered the professional ranks. His goal is to become Davie Moore's manager at the professional level, and to give him better opportunities than he had to turn into a champion professional boxer. The weight class Davie is fighting in is where the biggest payouts will come from. Thanks to professional boxers like Sugar Ray Leonard, Tommy (Hitman) Hearns, (Marvelous)Marvin Hagler, and (hands of stone) Roberto Duran to name a few, for their ability to attract boxing fans from all over the world. These boxers created boxing analysts that viewed boxing as a work of art. This generation of boxers created a demand in the boxing sports world. These fighters contributed to an explosion of multi-million dollar pay days. Leon believed that Davie can one day be a world champion. I had the opportunity to see Davie Moore box as an amateur, and I totally agree with Leon, Davie already fights more like a professional than an amateur.

I remember this car ride traveling to Madison Square Garden arena in Manhattan from the Morrisania Youth Center Bronx, New York like it was yesterday. Leon continued to tell his life experience as a professional boxer and how it negatively impacted on him, and his boxing career. He has ill feelings about his very bad managers and coaches, and their terrible decision making. Davie suddenly interrupted us sitting in the front seats, and asked, "do you have any cassette tapes by Stevie Wonder?" I said, "yes I so happen to have Stevie Wonders most recent album on tape and played it during the car ride. The album title is, "Songs in the Key of Life" it's a culmination of Stevie Wonders classic period albums. Stevie Wonder still is one of my favorite artists, this album was released on September 28, 1976. Once the sweet voice of Stevie Wonder began singing, everyone in the car was silent and was enjoying the music. It seems that we all got into our zones and began meditating. At least I did. I was reflecting back to when this whole journey began. "The phone call by plain clothes NYPD officer to verify Jimmy's alibi, my commitment to help Jimmy because I wanted to provide some kind of community service and help a street kid and comrade soldier. I threw my hat in the circle to be the good Samaritan and help Jimmy search for an escape. I did this to help him pursue a positive lifestyle with a career filled with love for humanity. I'm aware that once this tournament is over, he faces the gritty backdrop of poverty, burning tenement buildings, crime, street gangs, and homelessness. These real-life concerns left him no choice but to battle his inner emotions in a boxing ring. Hopefully after this journey the unavoidable lifestyle that illuminates his surroundings of his life will dissipate, or maybe non-exist. As I mentioned previously about Jimmy, he is special, because he already understands that life has more to offer than the one, he is being dealt. That first step to commit was very important, and now he gets his chance to use his incredible gifted fighting skills to score another victory to make this entire journey one huge success for him. I hope for the thousands of youths that picked the wrong path after surrounding themselves with their social demons find a positive path in their endeavors.

If Jimmy wins tonight, one day when I'm living my golden years, retired from the military, I will write a book to tell this South Bronx story.

We have arrived at the Madison Square Garden; this is the place for a boxing fan to be tonight for the finals of the 51st Golden Gloves boxing tournament. This night brought out a crowd of 20,366 boxing fans, the largest to watch this amateur event since 1968. This is a televised sports cable match, so millions of boxing fans will be watching from the comfort of their homes.

As all amateur boxers with their coaches and handlers began filling the locker rooms, suddenly, a local very familiar sports person TV personality comes into the locker room to congratulate all the amateur boxers for making it into the New York Daily News Golden Gloves Championship match. It is "Gentleman" Gerry Cooney,

Cooney won two New York Golden Gloves Championships, the 1973 160-lb Sub-Novice Championship. Cooney trained at the Huntington Athletic Club in Long Island, New York. His amateur record consisted of 55 wins and 3 losses. In 1981, he defeated former world heavyweight champion Ken Norton by a knockout just 54 seconds into the 1st round with a blisteringly powerful attack. This broke the record set in 1948 for the quickest knockout in a main event. Jerry Cooney announced in the locker room, "I want to congratulate all of you for the hard work, and commitment that you had to withstand to make it to the finals championship match. After Cooney's announcement, the entire locker room of fighters and handlers cheered and applauded him while he personally went around to greet all the boxers and their coaches. He approached every fighter and congratulated each one.

When he reached Jimmy and I he spoke about Jimmy's perseverance to make it to the finals, and wished him good luck in tonight's fight.

Jimmy Gomez vs. Fernando Linares was the first match of the night. Jimmy's hands were all bandaged and taped up, and the boxing gloves were tied, I put a light coat of Vaseline on his face, and Jimmy begins his shadow boxing, and boxing footwork in place to warm up his body before the fight begins. Suddenly a tournament representative shouts, "first up Jimmy Gomez versus Fernando Linares begin your walk towards the ring." Jimmy looks warm with beads of sweat running down his forehead. During the walk down the path towards the ring, a spot light beams on Jimmy Gomez, boxing fans began cheering, and yelling for Jimmy, it is definitely an exhilarating feeling for Jimmy to walk this walk towards the Main Stage of Madison Square Garden ring. One of many thoughts that ran through me at the time was, "I never mentioned to Jimmy or anyone else about my phone call with NYPD officer Smith. He said, during Jimmy's street fighting episode against gang members that robbed a senior woman's hand bag. Jimmy knockdown two gang members that outweighed him by at least 50 pounds." I always kept that information to myself, it helped me be aware of Jimmy's punching power and his perseverance. I got to see his punching power unfold a few times in the ring during his victory matches in this tournament. His punching power is for real, when he gets mad, or when he falls behind. Jimmy has not overused that hidden ability until it's the right time. The fighters meet in the center of the ring to go over the boxing rules. The referee reminds them that he went over the rules to all of the fighters, and asks them if they have any further question about the rules. Both fighters said, "no." The referee said, "ok, let's have a clean fight, protect yourselves at all times, and during the fight listen to all of my instructions at all times. Touch gloves, and good luck to both of you." Jimmy and Fernando touch gloves and return to their corner waiting for the 1st round bell to ring. I gave Jimmy a last-minute reminder, "protect yourself, he has a long reach." The bell rings, and both fighters meet in the center of the ring, and Fernando starts by throwing long left jabs, right crosses landing square on Jimmy's face. Fernando keeping as far away as possible to Jimmy's inside punching power. By now, all finalists knew more about their opponents' abilities, the word gets out about their opponents. Fernando, is jabbing and landing his punches, and Jimmy can't find a way to make contact with him. Fernando is on his bicycle, keeping outside and away from Jimmy's punching power. The problem is Fernando's punches when they reach

Jimmy, they are not strong enough to hurt him, but they do make contact to his body and score points. I yelled out, “Get inside Jimmy, start punching inside, and Jimmy begins punching and moving in, in doing so Fernando delivers two hard punches a left and a right to Jimmy’s jaw, and because Fernando is taller, he has to bend his head down to deliver punches because of Jimmy’s short stature. Jimmy showed Fernando no sign that those punches hurt him, but Jimmy had an opportunity for Fernando to feel Jimmy’s punching power. When Jimmy landed a left hook and a right cross, that landed directly on Fernando’s jaw, Fernando felt that he needed to step back against the ropes and counter punch Jimmy’s offensive attack. It now turns into a war; they were both punching for their life’s. It was a war; the crowd were on their feet cheering not for anyone individually, but to see two fighters giving it their all. They both were trying for a first-round knockout. I heard Fernando handler yelling to him, “get off the ropes,” but Jimmy’s powerful and fast punches did not allow Fernando to move off those ropes. The bell rings to end round one. Jimmy came back to his corner, and he asked, “Is this blood on my gloves his blood?” I told Jimmy, “It’s just your nose bleeding, it’s an easy fix just like we did many times at the gym”, nose bleeds look worse than what it is.” During the 1-minute rest period, I pinched the top of his nose with enough pressure to compress it against the cartilage, and had him take deep breaths from his mouth to lower his heart rate and slow down the outflow of the blood, this usually does the job, and in this case it worked. In the meantime, I told Jimmy, “he is connecting on your face too many times, keep your guard up. how do you feel? Are you ok?” Jimmy nods his head, yes. The audience is still cheering, the crowd noise is extremely loud. I told Jimmy, “Pace yourself, you don’t have to turn this into a war if you just time your counter punches, and hit him with your, big gun right hand." Jimmy said, "that's the only way I could get to him is when I turn it into a war." I said, "ok, when you go inside deliver an uppercut, he drops his head when he fights. Keep your guard up, when you throw your punches." Chip said, "your leaving your right hand down too low, keep it up by your face, be ready to block his counter punches. Protect your face, keep your guard up at all times." The bell rings for the beginning of round 2. Fernando gets on his bicycle and starts the same way he did the 1st round. Fernando delivers two quick jabs, and with his long arms connects with both of them, and quickly backs away to avoid Jimmy's counter punches. It looks like Fernando changed his fight plan. It seems to be working for Jimmy as Fernando backs away Jimmy finds his way inside and throws a left hook to his stomach, but with Fernando's quick foot speed avoids most of Jimmy's counter punches. Jimmy knows the only way he knows how to beat his opponent is to turn it into a street fight. Halfway through the 2nd round Fernando is looking like he is winning. I saw the discouraging look Jimmy was displaying, but I've seen that look before until discouragement turns into controlled rage. I yelled out, "Get inside and fight." Suddenly Jimmy grabbed both of Fernando's arms to take a breather, and muscled Fernando against the ropes. The referee broke them up, and said to the fighters, "come on let's fight." Jimmy went back to what he knows well, street fighting. He and Fernando were just swinging it out, suddenly, the entire 20 thousand plus boxing fans at the Garden came to their feet roaring for their fighters. It became a slugfest, just a who can knockout out who first, both fighters were landing. About 25 seconds remaining in the 2nd round, Fernando showed signs of exhaustion, but Jimmy's punching power and determination out pointed

Fernando, and at times landed very hard punches that would have dropped his previous opponents to the canvas. Fernando showed toughness and heart. The bell rings to end the 2nd round. The crowd still on their feet cheering and applauding mostly to let the boxers know that they were enjoying this fight. While Jimmy was walking to our corner, he got disoriented and began walking to a neutral corner. I yelled out to Jimmy, "This way Jimmy, wrong corner." The crowd still on their feet applauding, and roaring with appreciation for such a great boxing performance by both fighters. When Jimmy finally realized that he was in a neutral corner he appeared disoriented. He looked up and saw chip and I waving him back to his own corner. He looked extremely exhausted; perspiration was draining from everywhere. While he was walking towards his corner. I soaked a sponge fill of water and threw it towards his face to begin cooling him down, hopefully to cool him down in time for the 3rd and final round. When he sat on his stool, I cooled him down with more water, and asked him to sip some water from his water bottle for hydration. I asked Jimmy, “How do you feel?” He said, “my face hurts a little, this guy hits hard, but I could beat him.” Knowing Jimmy’s very strong determination and being this close to a victory, I said to him, “you turned this fight into a war, now you need to finish off this war and become the champ. Get in there and give it all you got. You have to reach way down this time Jimmy.” Before the bell rang, he was staring directly at his opponent, yes that stare that puts him in his combat zone. Bell rings for the 3rd and final round. Both fighters showing outstanding sportsmanship met in the center of the ring to tap gloves to show each other respect. The crowd appreciated their sportsmanship tap of gloves. They both worked extremely hard to get to this 3rd and final round. Fernando who trains out from a suburban gym of Yonkers, New York compared to Jimmy's gym surroundings who was born and raised in the tough streets of the South Bronx.

Jimmy begins by starting his war, but Fernando's foot work seemed to spring back, and just began doing what works for him. Jab and connect and quickly back away. Jimmy looked at the referee and gestured by raising both arms, while in the center of the ring. He tells the referee, "he is not fighting" the crowd began jeering, wanting the fighters to get back to mixing it up. With that Fernando met Jimmy in the center of the ring and began the throwing left and right crosses, Jimmy stayed calm and made himself a smaller target by lowering his head, both hands guarding his face, he advanced quickly and threw 2 powerful uppercuts that landed directly on Fernando's chin. When The 2nd uppercut landed on Fernando's chin, it drove his head back, which made the entire crowd stand to their feet, hoping to witness a fighter land on the canvas. The crowd stood up waiting to see if Fernando would hit the canvas, and when they saw that he didn't the crowd sounds were cheers and jeers. At this point the crowd had their personal selections who they wanted to win. Those punches backed Fernando to the ropes exactly where Jimmy is most successful. With Fernando back to the ropes the punches were flying, the crowd back up on their feet roaring and hoping for a knockdown. Fernando and Gomez were giving the boxing fans what they paid to see. The two best fighters making it to the final match at Madison Square Garden. The crowd cheering helps the fighters give it their all. They were like boxing robots nonstop, just left and right crosses, the technical fight was gone, it was a war. It seemed that both fighters were landing their punches, and about 30 seconds remaining in the final round, both fighters were showing signs of exhaustion. Their punches became sluggish, there was a point that they both took a four second breather and separated. Both corner handlers yelling out, keep punching. Both fighters continued to punch. Fernando caught Jimmy with a big wild left hand that landed on his jaw. I saw the discouraged gesture in Fernando when Jimmy quickly responded back with a barrage of accurate punches to his face that were unanswered by Fernando. Jimmy got this second wind to end the fight. Jimmy landed the most punches at the end, and a lot of them were power punches. The bell rang that ended the 3rd and final round. What a fight, two outstanding competitors just laying it all on the line, an incredible, entertaining fight, that was filled with heart, bravery, and toughness. The crowd on their feet the entire 3rd round. The judges go to their score cards to tally up the final decision. The bell rings a few times to get the audience attention, as the ring announcer gets the microphone that drops from the ceiling in the center of the ring. The referee is holding both Gomez and Fernando's glove in the center of the ring getting ready to raise the winner's hand. The ring announcer announces, "for the winner of the 1977 Golden Gloves championship fight out of the Morrisania Youth Center Gym Bronx, New York. Jimmy Gomez!" The referee raises Jimmy's arm, and the crowd all cheered for his victory. It was a close fight but Jimmy reached down deep inside in the last round, and gave a little more at the end, for the victory. To make a successful ending to Jimmy's journey so perfect, the New York Daily News captures and posted the next morning photos of Jimmy Gomez's victory championship match with action photos of the fight, and our final celebration bear hug leap, I photo titled it: "Leap of Trust."

What an adventure this journey turned out to be, Jimmy was looking for guidance in all the wrong places, stuck in an environment where he could have end up dead or in jail. He wore most of the same civilian clothes whenever I saw him off military duty. He was unemployed and probably on food stamps, not sure, and lived in the hood. Those are circumstances that he did not let dictate his life. He did not become a product of his environment. He became aware that he can control his destiny. He became aware that he could be the man that he was intended to be. He became aware that there was only one path he needed take with the people he trusted to help him. Jimmy decided to take the leap of trust, and opened up to others, and his whole life began opening more doors and opportunities. Boxing is discipline, work ethics, responsibilities, and lifelong skills -- and that's exactly what Jimmy Gomez learned in this three-month J

journey. I hope and pray today that Jimmy used this journey as a spring board to get him his social freedom he so earnestly deserves, to include a lifestyle of good health and happiness.

DAILY NEWS

NEW JERSEY

GLOVES SLUGDOWN

De Vorce, Vilella Win 2d Gloves Title

The Golden Moment

The New York Daily News captured terrific action photos of the fight. These photos filled the sports page the next morning. It also captured Jimmy leaping into Ron's arms for the final bear hug victory celebration.

Ron Sardanopoli

Jimmy Gomez and Ron Sardanopoli displaying Jimmy's 1977 Championship Golden Gloves award. Jimmy said, "I will wear this around my neck for the rest of his life."

Jimmy "Big Gun " Gomez, “Big Gun”, a nickname given to him by the sports writers to connect his punching power to his military occupation which is an Artillery Cannoneer. Gomez and Ron Sardanopoli with a 105 MM Artillery Gun in the backdrop.

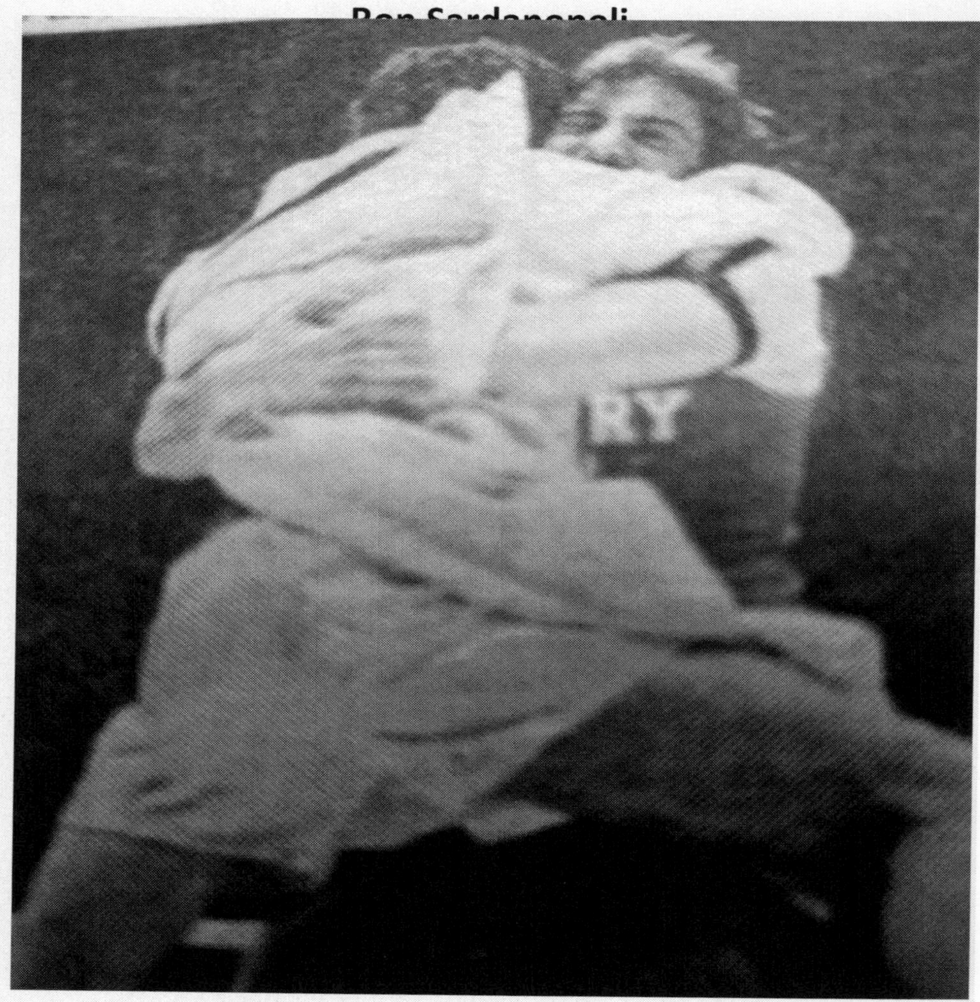

This is the final leap and bear hug by Jimmy Gomez at Madison Square Garden on March 11, 1977 to celebrate Jimmy Gomez's Championship Golden Gloves victory. The title for this photo is, Leap of Trust

Epilogue

By winning the 1977 Golden Gloves Championship Jimmy Gomez got an invitation to fight in the 1977 Chicago Golden Gloves. If Jimmy wins that match in Chicago, he would be on his way to Moscow and hopes to pull the lanyard and show his (big guns) at the 1980 Olympics. Jimmy turned it all down because he no longer wanted to fight. He shared earlier on during his journey that he was going to be a Goldens Glove Champion, and then he will never fight again. When he won the Golden Gloves Championship, he reminded me of this very sentiment once again. After winning the Golden Gloves Championship, he wanted to leave the sport of boxing as a winner, and he said, "I will wear this award-winning golden glove around my neck for the rest of my life." It's his reminder that he will succeed in all of life's challenges, and crossroads that come his way in his future endeavors. Life went on for Jimmy since that night at Madison Square Garden. Jimmy Gomez got his high school GED diploma and landed a fulltime job as a McDonalds store manager. He also contributed honorably as an American citizen soldier by completing his military obligation of six years with the New York Army National Guard, and was awarded an honorable discharge. I lost contact with Jimmy soon after, Jimmy should be about 62-years old today. I have done many searches before publishing this book in hopes to contact him, but there was no luck finding him. His incredible ability to have this very strong will to survive, a person that don't give up easy, or maybe never. The backdrop of his social battles of this decade in the South Bronx with social poverty, the burning buildings, street gangs and drugs. He seemed to live these years like he was not aware that these horrific surroundings even existed, or maybe he thought everyone in our country lived the same as him. This story is an inspirational treasure for Jimmy or anyone else that feels the odds are against them. After Jimmy's victory that night, he and I stayed to support his Morrisania Youth Center gym stable mates that were on the same card with him. Kenny Mitchel (Jimmy's sparring partner) lost his final match that night, while Davie Moore won his second New York Golden Gloves Championship match and went on to fight in his first Chicago Golden Gloves tournament and won. Johnny Hayes from the Morrisania Youth Center who fought out of the light heavyweight division lost his battle against a two-time Golden Gloves Champion Paul Christiani a United States Army West Point Cadet.

Leon, Chip, Davie, and Kenny from the Morrisania Youth Center gym, made us feel that we were part of a special group of serious contenders. We all developed very good relations during our stay at the Morrisania Youth Center in the Bronx. They all were not just mediocre coaches and future club fighters, these boxers and coaches, all were extraordinary. For Instance, Kenny Mitchel who was Jimmy Gomez sparring partner during his training days, became a world champion professional boxer his professional boxing career started in 1981 and in 1989 he captured the newly created and vacant World Boxing Organization Super Bantamweight title with a win over his challenger Julio Gervacio. An accomplishment that required so much training, and dedication, just to think that his boxing developed in a small deteriorated Morrisania Youth Center building in the South Bronx. Kenny spared over 70 rounds with Jimmy Gomez and eventually Jimmy's improvements helped Kenny Mitchell's development.

Leap of Trust

Leon Washington (Davie Moore's coach) moved to the Morrisania section of the Bronx, where Leon arrived from Santee, S.C., at age 10. He had come north to meet his father, only to see him pass away at Christmas. He stayed in the Bronx and did all his fighting in the streets until the age of 18. Leon got into the gym to avoid getting in trouble in the streets of the South Bronx. He became a very good professional middle weight boxer. He felt he was not managed and coached well when he became a professional boxer. People often told him, he could have been a middleweight champion of the world with the right manager, the right trainer, at the right time and the right place. When Leon first met Davie Moore at the Morrisania Youth Center, he coached Davie to become a very good amateur boxer. He knew immediately that, if Davie was managed the right way, he could be a champion at the professional level. Boxing champions in

Davies generation and weight class would bring in a very wealthy salary for Davie, and for himself. With Washington's management and boxing experience, coupled with Davies outstanding athletic physical and mental boxing abilities, both can land themselves a handsome payday. The boxing days of Sugar Ray Leonard, Roberto Duran, Thomas "Hit Man" Hearns, and let's not forget "Marvelous" Marvin Hagler paved the way to bring in large salaries for the top contenders. According to Leon, Davey Moore is very capable of reaching that milestone. Leon became Davie Moore's manager when Davie became a professional fighter.

Davie Moore was born in the South Bronx, N.Y., Moore won five Golden Gloves titles in New York and made the 1980 U.S. Olympic team that never competed in Moscow because of a boycott. Davie accomplished all his amateur success under the coaching tutelage of Leon Washington. He turned pro and won the World Boxing Association

Junior-Middleweight title in his ninth fight by stopping Tadashi Mihara in the 6th round in 1982. Moore retained his title three times. Roberto Duran who was pound for pound one of the greatest Junior Welterweight boxers of all time. Duran signed a contract to fight Davie Moore at Madison Square Garden in New York City. This boxing match was for Davie Moore's World Boxing Association Junior Welterweight Championship belt. I was there that evening to support Davie, and to witness Davie Moore take on one of the greatest fighters of all time, Roberto Duran, his nickname is, "Hands of Stone." Duran earned that nickname for the knockout power he brought to the ring. The match was close until Robert Duran accidentally punched Davie where the thumb of his boxing glove went into Davie's eye. Davie's eye swelled and closed, he lost sight in that eye during the remainder of the fight, and could no longer see in that eye. When Roberto Duran saw that Davies eye closed and was in trouble, Roberto always known to be a dominant finisher went in to deliver his world renown, crushing powerful punches. Davie Moore was beat this night on June 1983, when he was stopped in the 8th round. Davie Moore was still a top ten contender and was getting boxing contracts that maintained his financial status as a professional fighter. If he managed his money well, financially he would be set for the rest of his life.

Davie Moore's life took a sudden devastating turn. I picked up the evening newspaper and to read about the sad news. They reported that, Former WBA Junior-Middleweight champion Davey Moore was killed on a Friday when an unoccupied vehicle rolled down his driveway and ran over him as he tried to stop it. He was 28 years old. Moore's trainer, said, "Moore slipped on the wet ground while trying to stop the vehicle after it broke loose. Moore was then dragged downhill under the vehicle." Police said, "Moore's wife, summoned Officers and emergency medical technicians found Moore pinned under a Dodge Raider." Dispatcher said, "A tow truck was called to the Moore's' home and lifted the vehicle off him." Moore was taken to a local hospital where he was pronounced dead on June 3rd 1988. An autopsy showed Moore died of asphyxiation caused by a compressed chest. I was shocked and saddened when reading this news, my mind was running on a rollercoaster of different emotions, in complete disbelief to read about the passing of Davie Moore. May Davie rest in peace, God bless his soul, and blessings to his family that were left behind.

Chip was a seasoned corner man that in my eyes was the corner stone to the Morrisania Youth Center gym. He represented every fighter who was willing to train in that gym. Before, during and after tournament fights, Chip tried to always be there to help all the amateur boxers and their trainers during their boxing training at the gym and tournaments. Chip treated his service with complete compassion, and dedication to the sport of boxing and to the underprivileged youths of the South Bronx. He always offers youths an alternative to being on the street, one that teaches them lifelong skills. In turn, those people appreciate having a seasoned coach in their corner. "I love boxing," Chip once shared with me. He was a street fighter, who became a professional boxer, and learned all of the ingredients needed to become a mature young, humble, and respectable man in our society. Chip once shared with me, "I love working with the youths and seeing them progress." When he speaks, sincerity wreaks through his words.

Since leaving the boxing profession career, Chip attained fulltime employment as a source for income. He has volunteered for more than 35 years to helping street kids in various boxing programs in nearby New York City locations. He understood the structure of a boxing gym, and their street kids that come to learn.

Chip once told me, "I had worked in other boxing clubs before I visited the Morrisania Youth Center, and it was crazy, there are four or five coaches with their own little groups of boxers doing their own thing. Here in Morrisania Youth Center, everyone learns the same skills [and] everyone is on the same page. There is no preferential treatment, and that's what I instill in this gym." As I witnessed under Chips tutelage that many Morrisania Youth Center fighters have earned championship titles, and some of them became professional fighters, and World Boxing Associations Champions.

I really felt fortunate to use the Morrisania gym to help Jimmy, the sport of boxing under Chips tutelage was an important ingredient to Jimmy's success. Even though this gym appeared to be ready to tumble or be torched, while it was standing. It was a treasure for the inner-city youths, and volunteer coaches. This gym facility showed the youths the keys to life. The tools that Chip passed on to the many amateur boxers and coaches were educational. I learned how to be a boxing coach from somebody with more than 35 years of experience. Boxers are not allowed to continue on to circuit training or sparring until they demonstrate they can follow instructions and focus. Chip was very interested only to work with disciplined youths that come from various backgrounds. Sometimes street thugs were not accepted into Chips world. Those that thought they were not going to take any discipline from Chip, and to take a swing at him lost more than they thought. Once Chip puts up his boxing guard to block the thug's punches, and I've witnessed this a couple of times, half the gym boxers that were trained by Chip and treated Chip like a father were all over the thugs. They were thrown out the front door and were never allowed back in. Boxing gyms brings in all walks of life, I saw how Chip dealt with the youths and how he affects the youths. It's not always a happy ending, it's just giving someone a chance, and some guidance. Most street kids want discipline, structure, and a chance. Chip succeeded in delivering those very essential needs.

About the Author

Ron Sardanopoli is an adjunct professor retired, a career Army Chief Warrant Five-CW5 Officer retired, veteran, writer, and a non-fiction author of the book *Leap of Trust.* Ron's 36 years of military service opened up a treasure chest of experiences and journeys ranging throughout his years of service. His interest and focus are his riveting experiences that were surrounded by multicultural and inspirational people and events. Ron completed his graduate studies from the State University of New Paltz, New York with a Master's of Professional Studies degree in Humanistic/Multicultural Education. He also worked as an Adjunct Professor at Dutchess Community College, New York. All of his classroom work was created in an experiential workshop format to enhance the creative learning of potential supervisors. He also provided motivational lectures to Blue Chip corporations, and local businesses.

Ron lives and writes at his home in Myrtle Beach, South Carolina. He enjoys walking the beach in the morning with his wife Linda to catch the sunrise, and take in the ocean air. It's his way to jump start the day in a blessed life.

Made in the USA
Columbia, SC
27 January 2020

87194942R00155